THE DIABETIC AIR-FRYE

1500 Days Of Tasty And Super Easy Recipes To Help You Manage Your Diabetes While Enjoying Your Favorites Foods.
30 Days Meal Plan Included

Mackenzie Geller

Table of Contents

Introduction

Like a conventional oven, an air fryer can bake and roast. However, it differs from a standard oven in that it is equipped with heating elements on top, resulting in a more environmentally friendly cooking method with fewer oil splatters and a higher temperature. In contrast to an oven, which uses radiant heat from a large, enclosed heating element, an air fryer preheats food by circulating hot air from a powerful fan located at the top of a smaller, enclosed cooking compartment. If it doesn't make a clean getaway, the smoke from the fire should mold the inside of your device. The meals are placed in a basket-shaped fryer, and when turned on, hot air rushes down and over them.

Heat causes air to expand and cool. This process, known as convection, causes hot air to rise, cooking whatever is at the bottom of whatever is being cooked. The next part of the design is the basket, which functions similarly to a conventional oven's pan or cookie sheet by allowing hot air to circulate freely around the food.

Air fryers are so versatile that they can be used to cook almost any dish. There might be something for everyone, from frozen chicken wings and homemade French fries to roasted greens and freshly baked cookies. In recent years, this tool's popularity has increased, and now nearly 40% of homes in the United States have one. In most cases, a dishwasher can be used to clean a stove. As opposed to traditional frying, which introduces more unhealthy fats and energy, air frying is healthier. Therefore, diabetics have a greater preference for air-fried meals than they do for traditionally fried ones. Air fryers come in a wide variety of designs, sizes, and pricing points. It consists of a drawer to store food and a basket or grate to hold the food at an appropriate height. Inadequate heat dissipation from the heating element results in overheated oil or fat. Because an air fryer cooks with a significantly lower amount of fat than conventional techniques, it shouldn't have any unusual effects on diabetics. Because fat does not raise blood sugar levels in the same way that carbs do, people with type 2 diabetes should be able to eat air-fried foods without worrying about their blood sugar levels spiking too high. The air fryer uses hot air to completely cook whatever is inside. An air fryer's heating element and fan are located on its top panel; the fan keeps air moving over the element to heat it. Keep in mind that using an air fryer won't magically transform unhealthy foods into nutritious powerhouses. The ability to use discretion and good judgment when using it is not lost. Always check ingredient labels and see a dietician to learn what goes into your meals.

What is Diabetes?

Both type 1 and type 2 diabetes are serious conditions.

Type 1 diabetics are unable to produce their own insulin. If you have type 2 diabetes, the situation is a little different. Either the insulin you generate is ineffective or you can't make enough of it. Both of these illnesses are very serious despite their differences.

Some pregnant women will develop gestational diabetes, a different form of the disease. Type 3c and Latent Autoimmune Diabetes in Adults (LADA) are just two of many extremely uncommon forms of diabetes.

All forms of diabetes are characterized by a rise in blood glucose levels caused by an inability to adequately transport glucose into the body's cells. Many health issues can arise from having an excessive amount of glucose in your blood. For starters, it causes diabetes symptoms.

Diabetes, in whatever form it takes, is always characterized by an excess of blood glucose (sugar). But glucose is a necessity for everyone. This fuel is essential to our survival. Glucose is derived through the digestion of ingested carbohydrates. Additionally, the glucose is absorbed into the bloodstream. Insulin is a hormone that is essential to human survival. Insulin is produced by our pancreas and is responsible for transporting glucose from our blood into our cells, where it may be used as fuel.

High blood glucose levels are associated with long-term harm to the heart, eyes, feet, and kidneys. In medical terms, these are diabetic complications. However, given access to adequate medical care, people can recover and lead normal lives. This sort of issue is also extremely unlikely to occur. Examine the various issues and the measures you can take to lessen your likelihood of experiencing them. At present, type 1 diabetes cannot be prevented. Still unknown are the environmental triggers thought to initiate the process that leads to the death of insulin-producing cells in the body.

Although many factors contribute to the onset of type 2 diabetes, urbanization-associated lifestyle choices stand out as the most consequential. To name just two examples, these bad habits include eating poorly and not getting enough exercise. Physical activity and healthy eating have been shown to be effective in delaying or preventing the onset of type 2 diabetes in numerous studies conducted in a variety of geographic regions around the world. Physical inactivity and extended periods of sitting are hallmarks of the modern lifestyle. Through campaigns, education, and social marketing, community-based interventions can reach individuals and families and inspire them to engage in more physical activity at home, at school, and on the job. IDF advises engaging in some form of physical activity for at least 30–45 minutes on at least three days out of every week. In order to effectively prevent type 2 diabetes and its complications, it is crucial to view prevention from the perspective of the entire person's life. There is a crucial window of opportunity to prevent the onset of overweight and type 2 diabetes in early life, when eating and physical activity habits are established and the long-term regulation of energy balance may be programmed. Maintaining a healthy lifestyle can have positive effects on health even in old age.

Policies in trade, agriculture, transportation, and urban planning that prioritize the health of the population make it easier for individuals to make environmentally and socially responsible decisions. Everybody benefits from a healthier population when healthy lifestyles are encouraged in key social contexts like schools, workplaces, and homes. Regular exercise and healthy eating are two of the best ways to keep glucose, blood pressure, and lipids in healthy ranges.

Our best recommendations to prevent:

- Substituting water, coffee, or tea for sugary drinks like fruit juice, soda, or energy drinks.
- Three daily servings of vegetables, including dark green leafy vegetables.
- Consuming as many as three pieces of fruit per day.

- Picking a healthy snack like nuts, fruit, and unsweetened yogurt.

- Consuming no more than two drinks (using standard measuring cups) of alcohol per day.

- By avoiding fatty red meat and processed meat and opting instead for white meat, poultry, and seafood.

- Preferring peanut butter to other spreads like jam or chocolate.

- Avoiding saturated fats like butter, ghee, animal fat, coconut oil, and palm oil in favor of unsaturated fats like olive oil, canola oil, corn oil, and sunflower oil.

Is the air fryer healthy for diabetics?

Air fryers are preferable for diabetics because they do not necessitate the use of oil. In order to successfully prepare healthy meals in an air fryer, it is crucial to keep the food at the ideal frying temperature during the whole cooking process. Vegetables of all shapes and sizes can be cooked in an air fryer, not just meat.

People with diabetes can benefit from using air fryers since they reduce the demand for oil and the quantity of calories in deep-fried foods. As an added bonus, they allow people to enjoy "fried" foods without worrying about gaining weight or getting sick from the excessive grease. People who are diabetic can benefit greatly from this.

Using an air fryer allows you to prepare meals that are both healthier and lower in carbohydrates. However, deep-frying is risky because it produces more acrylamide than air-frying does. Consuming excessive amounts of acrylamide can lead to cancer and other health issues. Oils like rice bran oil are useful examples. It is a great option for diabetics due to its high concentration of monounsaturated fatty acids, which are known to lower cholesterol. Canola oil may be useful for diabetics, as suggested by the results of other studies. Consumption of foods containing these oils has been linked to a decreased threat of developing cardiovascular disease.

Olive oil, avocado oil, coconut oil, and sunflower oil are some alternates to these two oils if you have trouble finding them. Olive oil is often regarded as one of the healthiest oils for diabetics, which is something to think about. Air fryers, on their own, are not enough to make a difference in one's health. There is no assurance that the food that is produced by air fryers is appropriate for people who already have diabetes, despite the fact that the absence of oil in the cooking process offered by air fryers may lower the risk of acquiring diabetes in some people. It is essential to exercise caution when operating an air fryer, and the manner in which it should be operated will, to a large extent, be determined by the food that is being fried. In addition, diabetics are required to prepare their meals in advance and pay closer attention to the foods they put into their bodies. It is strongly suggested that one adhere to a diet consisting primarily of vegetables and lean proteins, and that one consume as little fruit, sugar, bread, rice, and other sweets as is humanly possible.

When utilizing an air fryer, it is important to make sure that the majority of your diet is comprised of these nutritious foods in order to prevent consuming an excessive amount of fat that comes from oil. You can only be as healthy as the food that you cook and eat on a regular basis. Choosing the appropriate foods for each of your meals is an important step in lowering the hazards that you expose yourself to. Always keep that in the back of your mind.

Breakfast

1. Super Tasty French Toasts

Serving Size: 4

Time Required for Preparation: 6 Minutes

Ingredients:

- To taste, add more or less maple syrup

- Three-quarters of a teaspoon of cinnamon

- French or Italian bread, 12 slices

- 2 eggs, beaten

- Vanilla extract, 1 teaspoon

- One cup of your favorite ripe berry; blueberries, strawberries, or raspberries

- Half a cup of milk (regular or almond) (soy or oat)

Directions:

Set the air fryer's temperature to 350 degrees.
In a large bowl, combine the milk, vanilla, eggs, and cinnamon by whisking the ingredients together.
Simply soak each piece of bread in the egg mixture until it is completely covered, then place it in a container lined with paper towels to drain.
Cook the French toast for about 4-6minutes on each side until golden brown.
Top the brown bread with maple syrup and fresh blueberries. Enjoy

Nutritional value per serving: Calories: 264, Fat: 7.5g, Cholesterol: 116mg, Protein: 8g, Carbohydrates: 46g, Sodium: 272mg, Fiber: 2.6g

2. Hard Egg

Serving Size: 3

Cooking Time: 18 minutes

Ingredients:

- 3 large eggs

- 1 bowl with water and Ice

Directions:

About 5 minutes before you start boiling water, fill the bowl with iced water and some ice. This will keep the egg nice and cold.
Bring the water to a boil and add the eggs straight from the ice water (don't worry, the hot water won't crack the eggs)
When the water is boiling, use a timer, and set it for 3.5 minutes. With the eggs in the pot, put a weight on them like a plastic plate, so they don't float up while cooking. They won't experience the annoyance of top-level bubbles anymore.
After 3.5 minutes, turn the eggs over with a spoon, then cook for another 3 seconds.
Let the eggs sit in the water
The eggs are cooked when there are no runny yolks anymore, and the whites are cooked but not too dry.
And voila, you have perfectly done eggs.
They are also great to eat on their own, with some salt, pepper, and garlic.

Nutritional value per serving: Calories: 93 Fat: 5g Cholesterol: 251mg Sodium: 99mg Carbohydrates: 0g Fiber: 0g Sugar: 0g Protein: 7g

3. *Prosciutto and Spinach Egg Cup*

Serving Size: 6

Cooking Time: 15 minutes

Ingredients:

- 6 slices prosciutto

- 6 eggs

- ½ cup baby spinach

- Pinch of salt

- ¼ teaspoon pepper

Directions:

Preheat your air fryer to 375°F. Spray or drizzle oil into the muffin pan. Each cup should have one piece of prosciutto inside it, pressed into the bottom and sides.

Place a teaspoon of spinach in each prosciutto cup, pressing lightly to secure.

Break an egg over the top of the spinach, distributing it among the cups.

Sprinkle with a pinch of salt and pepper.

Until the whites are firm and the yolks are still somewhat runny, bake the eggs in the air fryer for 10 to 12 minutes.

Immediately after step 7, take the food out of the pan and serve it.

Nutritional value per serving: 110 calories, 0.9 g of carbohydrates, 0.9 g of fiber, 8 g of fat, and 7.6 g of protein.

4. *Toasted Eggs with Cheese*

Serving Size: 2

Preparation Time: 16 Minutes

Ingredients:

- 4 Extra-Large Eggs

- 2 ounces of chopped smoked gouda

- Seasoning for everything bagels

- Salt and pepper to taste, preferably with Kosher salt

Directions:

First, crack eggs into a bowl and sort them. To make the whites stiff, beat them.
Second, in a separate bowl, blend the egg yolks, Everything Bagel seasoning, salt, and pepper until smooth. Gently incorporate the chopped Smoked Gouda.
Fourth, using roughly a tablespoon each muffin, transfer the mixture to mini-egg muffin pans.
Bake the cans at 400 degrees for 14 minutes in a single layer in an air fryer.
As soon as the timer goes off, carefully use a fork to pry the egg muffins out of the tins and transfer them to a serving tray.
When ready to serve, sprinkle a little pepper and Everything Bagel spice on top.

Nutritional value per serving: Fat 15 g, Protein 14 g, Carbohydrate 1 g, Fat 250 kcal

5. *Blueberry Muffins*

Serving Size: 3

Preparation Time: 5 Min

Ingredients:

- 1 cup almond flour

- A single serving of blueberries, or one cup

- 1 egg

- A quarter cup of milk

- Baking powder, 1 tsp.

- Two level tablespoons of erythritol powder

- One-third of a teaspoon of salt

Directions:

First, mix the powdered erythritol, almond flour, baking powder, salt, and milk together in a big basin. Combine all of the ingredients together. Make sure the mixture has been thoroughly mixed. Second, incorporate the blueberries into the mixture. Put the mixture into a silicon muffin tin. After setting the muffin pan inside the air fryer's tray or basket, let it heat up for around five minutes. In the area of 329 degrees Fahrenheit is where you want to be.
Five, your homemade Blueberry Muffins are done and ready to be eaten.

Nutritional value per serving: 9 grams of carbohydrates, 4 grams of sugar, 7 grams of protein, and 9.3 grams of fat in this dish.

6.   *Toasted Items with Savory Combination of Mashed potato and Ripe*

Serving Size: 4

Preparation Time: 15 Min

Ingredients:

- a sweet potato, weighing between three-quarters and one pound;

- 1 fresh, ripe avocado

- One Tablespoon of Olive Oil;

- One-fourth cup of cherry tomatoes

- a pinch of dried oregano;

- The right amount of salt and pepper

Directions:

Start by preheating the air fryer to a temperature of 400 degrees Fahrenheit.
Apply olive oil to one side of each sweet potato slice, then flip the slices over. Spread out in a single layer on a baking sheet covered in foil.
Put in the oven and bake for 6-10 minutes, or until a fork can be inserted without difficulty.
After the sweet potatoes have cooled, soften the avocado in a small bowl by mashing it with a fork.
Before serving, season with salt and pepper. Muddle the avocados together.
Top with chopped cilantro and cherry tomatoes for presentation. Enjoy

Nutritional value per serving: 185; protein: 2.8; carbohydrates: 25; fat: 7

7. *Granola Baked in an Air Fryer*

Serving Size: 4

Preparation Time: 10 Min

Ingredients:

- Half a cup of chopped almonds

- A single cup of rolled or old-fashioned oats,

- A pinch of salt, one teaspoon of cinnamon,

- Honey, about 3 tablespoons' worth

- The equivalent of two tablespoons of melted coconut oil,

- A single teaspoon of vanilla extract.

Directions:

The first step is to combine all of the ingredients in a bowl and stir them thoroughly.
Make sure the bottom of your air fryer tray is covered in parchment paper.
The third step is to transfer the mixture to the prepared tray and spread it out evenly. For this, a spoon will do just fine.
To make this dish, heat the oven to about 350 degrees Fahrenheit and cook the ingredients for about ten minutes.
Remove the granola from the air fryer's basket and spread it out to cool completely.
You can now serve the granola you made in the air fryer.

Nutritional value per serving: Vitamins and Minerals: 299 Foods containing 33 grams of carbohydrates Protein and Fiber Content: 5 and 7 Fat: 18 Sugar:15g

8. Avocado Rolls

Serving Size: 4

Preparation Time: 25 Min

Ingredients:

- 10 wrappers

- 3 thinly chopped avocados

- 1 sliced and chopped tomato

- Toss with a little salt and pepper if desired.

- 1 teaspoon of extra virgin olive oil

- 4 tbsp. chili powder

- dates and their sugar, 2 tbsp.

- 1 tbsp. oil from hemp seeds Vinegar with a high acid content

Directions:

Avocados may be mashed in a bowl Tomatoes, salt, and pepper should be added to the mixture and mixed thoroughly.
On top of it, place the wrappers and scoop mix.
Seal the edges by rolling them up and rolling them up again.
Cook for 5 minutes at 350 degrees Fahrenheit in your Air Fryer. In a bowl, combine the rest of the ingredients and serve with a dipping sauce, if desired. Enjoy!

Nutritional value per serving: Energy 422 kilocalories, Carbohydrates are 38 g per serving, Fat content is 15 grammes.

9.   *Super Oatmeal In Air Fryer*

Serving Size: 1

Preparation Time: 10 Min

Ingredients:

- 2 tablespoons of oat or almond flour

- Sugar equivalent of 1.5 teaspoons of stevia

- 14 teaspoon baking powder

- : Vanilla Extract, 14 tsp

- Unsweetened Almond Milk, 6 Tablespoons

- 12 cup of Quick Oats

- A Cinnamon Smear

- 3 tablespoons of fat-free Greek yogurt

Directions:

Start by greasing your air fryer. To make the quick oats, place the oats, stevia, unflavored collagen, cinnamon, and baking powder in a blender and blend on high for 30 seconds, or until smooth.

Third, in a bowl, combine the yogurt, vanilla extract, and milk.

After the dry oat mixture from step 2 has been poured into the bowl, the batter should be stirred until it is smooth. Put the batter in the air fryer's basket after you've transferred the smooth batter to the air fryer's tray.

Bake the batter at 350 degrees Fahrenheit for about 12 minutes. To prevent the oats from becoming dry in the middle, you should not cook them for too long, let it cook, then garnish.

Nutritional value per serving: 250; protein: 2.8; carbohydrates: 34; fat: 5

10. *Bacon And Corn*

Serving Size: 4

Preparation Time: 50 Min

Ingredients:

- 3 slices center-cut bacon

- 1 cup chopped red bell pepper

- 1 cup chopped onion

- 4 cloves garlic, minced

- 2 cup of fresh corn kernels (3-4 ears) (3-4 ears)

- 3 Tsp water, divided

- ½ Tbsp salt

- 1 Tsp all-purpose flour

- 2 cup of low-sodium chicken broth, divided

- ¼ cup dry white wine

- 8 ounces Yukon Gold potatoes, peeled and diced

- Five fresh thyme sprigs, plus additional leaves for garnish

- 1/4 cup of milk or cream

- A Half Tablespoon of Butter

- ½ Tbsp ground pepper

Directions:

Cook bacon in a big saucepan over medium warmness till crisp, eight to nine minutes. Place the bacon on a paper towel-lined dish, reserving the drippings in the pan (1 Tbsp). Break the bacon into small pieces and set it aside.

Toss in the onion, garlic, and bell pepper and simmer, turning frequently, for 6-8 minutes, or until the vegetables have softened and begun to brown. Put the bell pepper mixture into a medium bowl and put it aside. Put the corn, 2 tablespoons of water, and a pinch of salt into a skillet and simmer over medium heat, stirring frequently, until the corn is golden brown, about 4 to 5 minutes. Incorporate the last tablespoon of water, scraping the bottom of the pan to free any browned bits, and stir.

Put the pepper and onion mixture back in the pan. Sprinkle in the flour and cook for 1 minute, stirring constantly. Add the remaining 1/4 cup broth and wine and simmer for 1 minute, stirring often and scraping the bottom of the pan to release any browned bits. Add the potatoes and the last 3/4 cup of stock along with the thyme and stir. Produce to a boil while covered. The potatoes should be fork-tender after 15-18 minutes of simmering at a low heat.

Take out the thyme and throw it away. Put in a blender 2 cups of the soup. Take off the plastic insert in the lid (for steam to escape), set the cover level on the blender, and cover with a dish towel. Blend until silky (use warning while mixing warm liquids). Put the blended soup back in the pot. Add half a tablespoon of butter and stir. Serve in four dishes and season with pepper and the optional crumbled bacon and thyme leaves for garnish.

Nutritional value per serving: Energy 450 kilocalories, Carbohydrates are 46 g per serving, Fat content is 19 grammes.

Lunches and Salads

1. Chickpeas

Serving Size: 4

Preparation Time: 20 Min

Ingredients:

- 1 (15 oz.) can of chickpeas, drained and rinsed

- toasted sesame oil (1 1/2 tsp)

- 14 tsp smoked paprika

- 14 teaspoon of dried crushed red pepper

- 1/8 tsp of salt

- Spray oil for cooking

- Two wedges of lime

Directions:

Spread the chickpeas on several layers of paper towels. Dry the chickpeas on all sides by rolling them under the paper towels, then piling more paper towels on top and patting them dry.

In a medium bowl, combine the oil and chickpeas. Salt, crushed red pepper, and paprika must be used. Pour into a cooking foam air fryer basket. Cook in 12 to 14 minutes at 400 degrees F, shaking the basket occasionally until very well browned. Serve the chickpeas and lime wedges over the top.

Nutritional value per serving: 12 grams of carbohydrates, 4 grams of sugar, 7 grams of protein, and 9 grams of fat in this dish.

2. Shrimps

Serving Size: 4

Preparation Time: 10 Min

Ingredients:

- 1 pound peeled and deveined large shrimp, tails on

- 2 Tsp extra-virgin olive oil

- 2 Tsp lemon juice

- 2 cloves garlic, grated

- ½ Tbsp crushed red pepper, plus more for garnish

- ¼ Tbsp salt

- 1 Tsp minced fresh chives

Directions:

400°F must be maintained if an air fryer is cooked.

The shrimp, oil, lemon juice, garlic, crushed red pepper, and salt should all be combined in a medium bowl with the shrimp.

Using a slotted spoon, transfer the shrimp to the fryer basket. Cook the shrimp for around 5 minutes until they are opaque and pink. If desired, place in a serving dish and garnish with chives and extra red pepper flakes. Lemon slices work great.

Nutritional value per serving: 16 grams of carbohydrates, 8 grams of sugar, 14 grams of protein, and 7.3 grams of fat in this dish.

3. Lemon And Pepper Aioli

Serving Size: 4

Preparation Time: 15 Min

Ingredients:

- a pepper and a half,

- 1 tsp. avocado oil,

- vegan mayonnaise (about a half cup),

- a couple of tablespoons of pure, unfiltered lemon juice,

- a single minced garlic clove,

- 1 tsp. of finely chopped fresh parsley

- A pinch of salt and a pinch of pepper,

- Plus half of a pepper

Directions:

Vegan mayonnaise, freshly squeezed lemon juice, finely chopped fresh parsley, pepper, sea salt, and finely minced garlic should all be combined in a bowl and stirred until everything is evenly distributed. Reserve for a while so the flavors may mingle.

Turn on the air fryer and let it heat up for about three minutes, until it reaches 380 degrees Fahrenheit.

Spread the shishito peppers out in a single layer in the air fryer basket after tossing them with oil.

Broil for around four minutes in the air. When done, the peppers will have developed tiny blisters and softened slightly. Add two additional minutes of cooking time if it's still not done. Remove the food from the basket, season it with salt and freshly squeezed lemon juice, and serve.

Nutritional value per serving: Calories (218), carbs (5 g), fiber (2 g), sugars (3 g), protein (1 g), fat (20 g), cholesterol (10 mg), and salt (370 mg).

4. Bacon-Wrapped Asparagus

Serving Size: 8

Preparation Time: 10 Min

Ingredients:

- Approximately 1 bunch of asparagus
- Bacon, 1 lb (regular sliced not thick)

Directions:

Firstly, before using asparagus in the recipe, wash it and pat it dry with a dish towel, wrap a piece of bacon around each piece of tender asparagus; next, use a toothpick to secure the bacon-wrapped spears together.

Then cover the stems and bacon and cook them in an air fryer at 400 degrees Fahrenheit for about 12 minutes, or until the bacon is browned and the stems are firm. Drain on paper towels and season with salt after they've been removed from the pan.

Nutritional value per serving: 270 Calories; 19 G Fat; 59 mg Cholesterol; 949 mg Sodium; 1 G Carbohydrate; 0 G Fiber; 0 G Sugar; 18 G Protein.

5. *Zucchini Fries*

Serving Size: 4

Preparation Time: 10 Min

Ingredients:

- 2 zucchinis, medium in size
- 1 beaten big egg
- 13 cup almond flour
- One-half cup of grated parmesan
- tsp. of Italian seasoning
- Garlic powder, half a teaspoon
- A pinch of salt from the sea, about a quarter teaspoon
- A pinch of black pepper, equivalent to a quarter teaspoon
- One-fourth teaspoon of olive oil spray

Directions:

First, cut the zucchini in half lengthwise, and then slice each half into many sticks that are about half an inch thick and four inches long.

Mix together the almond flour, Italian seasoning, grated parmesan, garlic powder, black pepper, and salt in a bowl. Put the dish down, whisk the egg in a separate basin until it becomes foamy.

Dip the zucchini sticks in the egg, and then in the almond flour and salt mixture. The zucchini sticks need to be sprayed with extra virgin olive oil spray, after coating the zucchini sticks with the seasoning, place them in the air fryer's basket and cook them for about ten minutes at 400 degrees Fahrenheit.

Nutritional value per serving: 115 calories, 6 carbs, 8 grams of protein, 7 grams of fat, 400 milligrams of sodium, 1 gram of fiber, and 3 grams of sugar.

6. *Jalapeño Poppers, Lightly Fried*

Serving Size: 6

Preparation Time: 12 Min

Ingredients:

- Six medium jalapeos
- Four ounces of melted cream cheese
- Six to twelve slices of cooked bacon

Directions:

The first step is to cut the jalapeos into halves of equal length. The jalapeos must have their seeds removed. Wash the jalapeos thoroughly.

Second, slice the log of cream cheese into thin strips and stuff one piece into each pepper half.

Put the stuffed pepper on a baking sheet, stuff it with cheese, and then wrap it in bacon and secure it with a toothpick.

Cook the stuffed peppers in an air fryer by placing them in the appliance's basket. Check for any potential overlap and eliminate it.

Put the food in the air fryer and cook it at 370 degrees Fahrenheit for about 12 minutes, or until it's as crisp as you like it.

Nutritional value per serving: 80 calories, 2 grams of carbohydrates, 1 gram of fiber, 1 gram of sugar, 1 gram of protein, 7 grams of fat At 19 milligrams, cholesterol and 59 milligrams of sodium,

7. *Low Carb Fried Pickles*

Serving Size: 4

Preparation Time: 10 Min

Ingredients:

- One-fourth cup of grated Parmesan

- 2 eggs,

- 0.5 cups of almond flour,

- three dill pickle slices

- a pinch of salt, if you must.

Directions:

First, use cooking spray to coat the inside of the air fryer pan and the air fryer basket.

Put the two eggs in a bowl and put them aside.

Third, mix the ground almonds, salt, and parmesan cheese in a separate bowl.

After you have diced the pickles, you can roll them in the beaten eggs, after coating the pickles in the almond flour mixture, dredge them. Arrange the slices of pickle in a single layer in the air fryer.

Add the pan to the oven and cook for about five minutes at 360 degrees Fahrenheit. After turning the pickle slices, continue cooking for another 5 minutes.

Nutritional value per serving: 5 grams of carbohydrates, 1 gram of sugar, 2 grams of fiber, 84 milligrams of cholesterol, and 10 grams of fat in the entire serving. There are 9 grams of protein in a serving.

8. Okra Prepared In An Air Fryer

Serving Size: 8

Preparation Time: 13 Min

Ingredients:

- 1 pound of okra
- Olive oil, 2 teaspoons
- 1 teaspoon salt

Directions:

The first step in preparing the okra is to wash and pat it dry. Toss the okra that has been mixed with olive oil and salt.

Third, arrange the okra in a single layer in the air fryer's cooking basket. Air-fry at 400 degrees Fahrenheit for 13 minutes, shaking every 6 minutes, until the food gets the required crispiness.

Nutritional value per serving: 27 Calories 3.5 grams of carbohydrates, 1 gram of sugar, 2 grams of fiber, 1 gram of fat, and 1 gram of protein.

9. Tasty Pumpkin Seeds

Serving Size: 7

Preparation Time: 15 Min

Ingredients:

- 3/4 cups raw whole pumpkin seeds;
- 1/4 teaspoon garlic powder
- 1 tablespoon of olive oil
- 1/4 teaspoon of salt

Directions:

The pumpkin seeds should be strained before using. Rinse the seeds under cold water to get rid of the orange goop.

Third, place the cleaned seeds on a plate lined with paper towels. Next, place another double-layered paper towel on a flat surface and press down on the seeds to dry them.

Fifth, in a bowl, combine the seeds. Season the bowl with salt, garlic powder, and olive oil, then mix everything together thoroughly. Place the mixture in the basket of the air fryer.

Set the oven to 350 degrees Fahrenheit and cook for 15 minutes. While the basket is cooking, give it a light shake every so often. If you were to do this, the seeds would turn a golden brown color and become crisp.

You may now give your guests the delicious pumpkin seed dish you made in the air fryer.

Nutritional value per serving: Calories: 190, Fat: 16g, Carbohydrates: 5g, Protein: 10g, Sodium: 92mg, Fiber: 3g

10. Kale Chips

Serving Size: 5

Preparation Time: 10 minutes

Ingredients:

- 2 cups kale
- ½ tsp olive oil
- ¼ tsp salt

Directions:

Clean the kale by rinsing it under cold water and removing the tough center rib.

To dice, use a chef's knife.

Third, spread out in a single layer in the basket of your air fryer. Stir the olive oil and salt into the greens until it is well distributed. Cook in an air fryer for 5 minutes at 330 degrees Fahrenheit.

Take out of the air fryer and let it cool down.

Nutritional value per serving: of sodium, 2g of fat, 3g of protein, 5g of carbohydrates, and 2g of fat.

11. Beet Chips

Ingredients:

- 1 beet
- 1/4 teaspoon olive oil
- 1/4 teaspoon salt

Serving Size: 2

Preparation Time: 8 minutes

Directions:

The first step is to thoroughly clean the beets. To make slicing easier, cut off both ends of the root from the bulb. Second, slice the beets into uniformly thin slices using the mandolin.

The basket of an air fryer should be oiled before each use to prevent food from sticking. Arrange the beet slices in the basket in a single layer. Consider using salt if necessary.

Air fry at 300 degrees Fahrenheit for around 8 minutes.

Nutritional value per serving: 22, Fat grams: 1, Protein grams: 1 5g of carbs, 1g of protein, 1g of fat, 325mg of sodium, 1g of fiber, and 2.5g of sugar.

12. Cordon Bleu

Serving Size: 6

Preparation Time: 15 minutes

Ingredients:

- Bread crumbs (about a cup's worth of panko);

- A pound of deli ham cut into four slices;

- Chicken breast halves without the skin;

- One-fourth of a teaspoon salt;

- Two pieces of Swiss cheese that have been matured;

- Spray oil for cooking;

- A quarter of a teaspoon of pepper

The sauce is made by combining the following:

- One-fourth cup of dry white wine,

- 1/8 teaspoon salt,

- One Tablespoon Flour

- Shredded Swiss cheese, about 3 teaspoons' worth

- A half a cup of milk.

- Season with pepper.

Directions:

First, preheat the air fryer to a temperature of 365 degrees Fahrenheit.

Pepper and salt the chicken breasts, then place them in the Air Fryer at a temperature of 365 degrees Fahrenheit. Top each chicken breast with a piece of ham and a half a slice of cheese. Make sure the chickens are completely covered by folding the ham slice in half.

Finally, sprinkle some breadcrumbs. For a total of 7 minutes, keep cooking, in a small saucepan, whisk together the milk and flour for the sauce until smooth.

Bring to a boil, and simmer for a further two minutes, or until the mixture reaches the desired consistency.

Return the mixture to the pot and simmer for another three minutes, or until the cheese has melted and the sauce has thickened, after you have stirred in the cheese and wine in step.

Nutritional value per serving: 269 calories, 13 grams of carbs, 1.8 grams of sugars, 1 gram of fiber, 7 grams of fat, 81 milligrams of cholesterol, 522 milligrams of sodium, and 30 grams of protein from half a chicken breast.

13. *Air-Fried Fish and Chips*

Serving Size: 2

Preparation Time: 25 minutes

Ingredients:

- One potato
- A tablespoon of olive oil
- A pinch of salt, and a pinch of pepper

For the fish, you'll need:

- Haddock (around half a pound),

- 1 egg,

- 3 tbsp. of all-purpose flour,

- A pinch of pepper, two table spoons of water,

- Grated Parmesan cheese (one and a half teaspoons),

- One-third a cup of cornflakes, crushed

- Cayenne pepper for spice,

- 1/8 teaspoon of salt and tartar sauce (optional)

Directions:

Preheat the air fryer to 400 degrees Fahrenheit.
After you've peeled the potato, divide it into two pieces, each of which is 12 inches in length. Toss the pepper, salt, and oil together in a big basin. The potato is then dunked into the sauce.
Seasoned potato slices are placed in the air fryer's cooking basket and fried for around 5-10 minutes. Even out the potato distribution in the basket by moving them around, and keep them in the oven for another 5-10 minutes. Flour and pepper should be mixed together in a separate bowl.
To make number seven, separate a bowl and add the water to the egg while beating it.
Mix cornflakes, cheese, and cayenne pepper together in a separate bowl.
To prepare the fish for serving, season it with salt and then dredge it in the flour mixture. Apply the coating to both sides equally. Toss the breaded fish into the beaten egg, and ten, add it to the basin. Next, submerge in the cornflake slurry. After the fish has been coated, place it in the air fryer's basket and cook it until it is a light brown color, about 11 minutes. Be cautious of overcooking. Serve.

Nutritional value per serving: 33 grams of carbohydrates, 2.8 grams of sugars, 1 gram of fiber, 10 grams of fat, 87 milligrams of cholesterol, 499 milligrams of sodium, and 24 grams of protein in this dish.

14. *Flavorful Chicken*

Serving Size: 6

Preparation Time: 45 minutes

Ingredients:

- A dry massage, 1 tbsp.

- 3.5 pounds of whole chicken

- Salt (optional)

- Spray oil for cooking

Directions:

First, while the air fryer is preheating, raise the temperature inside to to 350 degrees Fahrenheit. Rinse the chicken off with water.

Third, pat the clean chicken with a paper towel to dry it completely. Use a dry rub to season the chicken all over, then add salt to taste. Spread the dry rub all over the chicken.

Spray the air fryer with cooking spray to keep food from sticking to the basket.

Cook the chicken for an hour, turning it over once, until it reaches an internal temperature of 165 degrees on both sides (see step 6). Depending on the size of the chicken, the cooking time may vary. You may now serve the full chicken you fried in the air fryer.

Nutritional value per serving: 269 calories, 1 gram of carbohydrates, 1 gram of fiber, 1 gram of sugar, 23 grams of protein, 21 grams of fat, 91 milligrams of cholesterol, and 90 milligrams of sodium.

15. In-Air Fryer Steak

Serving Size: 1-2

Preparation Time: 30 minutes

Ingredients:

- A New York Strip steak that is 8 ounces in size

- Steak Marinade for the Air Fryer

- Half a teaspoon of cumin

- Lime juice, 3 tbsp

- 1 tbsp. of olive oil

- Three teaspoons of low-sodium soy sauce

- The equivalent of one garlic bulb

Directions:

Combine all marinade ingredients in a bowl. Marinate the meat for half an hour at room temperature after adding it.
Second, get the air fryer up to temperature, preferably 400 degrees F.
Third, remove the steak from the marinade, shake off any excess, and put it in the air fryer. Put it in the oven for three minutes (medium rare)
Remove the pan from the stove and let it cool for about 10 minutes.
Serve by slicing into bite-sized pieces.

Nutritional value per serving: 701 Calories; 47 G Fat; 178 mg Cholesterol; 1140 mg Sodium; 13 G Carbohydrates; 1 G Sugar; 45 G Protein.

16. *Delicious Mushrooms*

Serving Size: 2

Preparation Time: 8 minutes

Ingredients:

- Cremini mushrooms, 8 ounces (clean & dry, halved)

- Soy sauce, 1 tablespoon

- Lemon juice, 1 tablespoon

- The powdered form of garlic, about half a teaspoon

- One-eighth of a teaspoon of black pepper (optional)

Directions:

Mix the mushrooms with the soy sauce, lemon juice, garlic powder, and pepper in a plastic bag or bowl.
Marinated mushrooms require 8 minutes in an air fryer set to 390 degrees Fahrenheit.
After 4 minutes have gone, give it a quick toss or stir.
Enjoy

Nutritional value per serving: 31 calories; 6.7 grams of carbohydrates; 1 gram of fiber; 2 grams of sugar; 2.9 grams of protein; 1 gram of fat; and 268 milligrams of sodium.

17.   *Cooking Carrots with an Air Fryer*

Serving Size: 6

Preparation Time: 12 minutes

Ingredients:

- 2 teaspoons of brown sugar

- One Tablespoon of Olive Oil

- 1 lb. Baby carrots (peeled and cut in half lengthwise)

- 1/2 teaspoon of smoked paprika

- 2 tablespoons of grated Parmesan

- Tarragon, dried, one teaspoon

- Half a teaspoon of salt

- 1/4 teaspoon ground pepper

Directions:

Air fryer temperature should be set to 390 degrees Fahrenheit.
In a large bowl, combine the carrots, cheese, oil, sugar, tarragon, paprika, salt, and pepper.
Add the carrots to the air fryer basket, and cook for 6 minutes.
Flip the carrots and cook 6 minutes more.
Enjoy

Nutritional value per serving: 66 Calories; Protein 1g; Carbohydrates 8.8g; Fiber 2g; Sugars 5.1g; Fat 2.7g; Cholesterol 1mg; Sodium 275mg;

18. *Air Fryer Eggplant*

Serving Size: 8

Preparation time: 30 minutes

Ingredients:

- 2 small eggplants (sliced 1/4-inch thick)

- 1/2 tsp. salt

- Half a cup of panko breadcrumbs (whole wheat)

- 1/4 cup flour (any kind)

- 1 tbsp. of finely chopped fresh parsley

- Two large eggs (lightly beaten)

- 1/4 cup grated Parmesan

- Spray olive oil for cooking

Directions:

Apply salt evenly to the eggplant slices and let them sit for 10 minutes.
Slices should be dried with a paper towel. Spread the flour out in a pie plate. Don't forget to get out another plate for the eggs.
In a second, smaller dish, combine the Italian seasoning and parmesan.
Coat the eggplant slice with flour, then the beaten egg, and finally the panko crumbs. Before dipping the egg into the panko, make sure it isn't dripping. Turn on your air fryer and set the temperature to 375 degrees F.
Line the air fryer's basket with the eggplant slices and spray them liberally with cooking spray.
Prepare the slices for cooking for about 12 minutes, or until they are golden brown on both sides.
Parsley and parmesan cheese are optional toppings for the air-fried eggplant slices.

Nutritional value per serving: 50 calories, 2.9 grams of protein, 8.1 grams of carbs, 2.3 grams of fiber, 2 grams of sugars, 2 grams of fat, 29 milligrams of cholesterol, and 210 milligrams of sodium.

19. *Tossing Beets and Feta in the Air Fryer*

Serving Size: 4

Preparation time: 20 minutes

Ingredients:

- Beets, one pound (trimmed, peeled and cut into 1-inch pieces)

- One tablespoon of olive oil, preferably extra-virgin

- Feta cheese, crumbled, 1/4 cup

- A pinch of salt, about a quarter of a teaspoon

- 1 tbsp. of chopped, fresh oregano (chopped)

- A quarter teaspoon of ground pepper

Directions:

The air fryer needs to be heated to 400 degrees Fahrenheit for 5 minutes. Toss the beets with the oil, salt, and pepper in a large basin.
Cook the beets for 10 minutes in a single layer in the air fryer basket.
Cook for another 7 minutes after turning the beets.
Take out of the basket and top with feta and fresh oregano;

Nutritional value per serving: 101 calories, 3 grams of protein, 10 grams of carbohydrates, 2.8 grams of fiber, 7.7 grams of sugars, 5 grams of fat, 7 milligrams of cholesterol, and 317 milligrams of sodium.

20. Red Potatoes, Fried

Serving Size: 8

Preparation time: 10 minutes

Ingredients:

• 1 teaspoon of dried oregano

• Two Tablespoons of Olive Oil

• Red potatoes, 2 lb (unpeeled and cut into wedges)

• Salt, half a teaspoon

• Include 2 cloves of garlic (minced)

• 14 tsp. pepper

Directions:

Prepare the potatoes by oiling them. Add seasonings (pepper, garlic, salt, and rosemary) and toss lightly to combine.
Cook for 10–12 minutes at 400°F, flipping once, until they are golden and tender in an air fryer.

Nutritional value per serving: 109 calories, 3.9 grams of fat, 148 milligrams of sodium, 16 grams of carbohydrates, 1 gram of sugar, 2 grams of fiber, and 2 grams of protein in a single serving (one cup).

21. Salmon With Lemon

Serving Size: 4

Preparation time: 12 minutes

Ingredients:

- Two pieces of salmon weighing 12 ounces each
- Four tablespoons of butter
- 2 lemon slices

Directions:

Put salmon fillets in the air fryer's basket. A lemon slice and pat of butter should be placed on top of each fillet. Prepare the food for 12 minutes at 400°F. The salmon is fully cooked when it flakes easily and has lost its pink hue. Arrange the salmon on a serving dish and top with lemon juice.

Nutritional value per serving: 438 calories, 31 grams of protein, 32 grams of fat, 158 milligrams of cholesterol, and 268 milligrams of sodium in addition to other nutrients.

22. *Turkey Fingers With Coconut Crunch*

Serving Size: 6

Preparation time: 20 minutes

Ingredients:

- 1.5 pounds of turkey breast tenderloins, cut into half-inch-wide strips;

- 1/2 cup of breadcrumbs that are dry;

- a half-teaspoon of salt

- Sesame oil, two teaspoons;

- two egg whites

- 1/2 cup of sweetened coconut flakes;

- cooking spray; and two tablespoons of toasted sesame seeds.

Directions:

Increase the air fryer's temperature to 400 degrees. Combine equal amounts of salt, coconut, bread crumbs, and sesame seeds to make a baking mixture. Mix the egg whites and oil together with a whisk in a different bowl.

Coat the turkey strips with an egg white mixture, then repeat the process by dipping them in the coconut mixture.

Spread the turkey evenly on the bottom of the air fryer's basket after coating it with oil.

After three to four minutes, flip the food and cook for an additional three to four minutes.

To make the sauce, put all of the ingredients in a pot and whisk them together. Then, bring the mixture to a boil and cook it for one to two minutes.

Arrange on plates, top with sauce, and top with lime wedges and zest.

Nutritional value per serving: 28 grams of protein, 301 calories, 8 grams of fat, 48 mg of cholesterol, 521 mg of sodium, 21 grams of carbohydrates, 4 grams of sugars, and 1 gram of fiber.

23. *Burger Fajitas*

Serving Size: 6

Preparation time: 20 minutes

Ingredients:

- 1 beef flank steak (about 1 pound)
- 1 jalapeno pepper (minced)
- 2 diced tomatoes (seeded)
- 3 tablespoons fresh cilantro (minced)
- 2 teaspoons cumin (ground) (divided)
- 6 8-inch-diameter warmed whole wheat tortillas;
- 1/2 cup red onions;
- 25 tablespoons lime juice
- 1/4 teaspoon salt (divided)
- One large onion, halved
- One avocado
- One lime

Directions:

In a small bowl, mix the chopped tomatoes, red onion, lime juice, jalapenos, and cilantro to make the salsa. Include 1 teaspoon cumin and 1/4 teaspoon salt. Place aside.

Use the salt and cumin that are still in the shaker to season the steak. Arrange the onion slices on a microwave-safe platter, and then microwave them on HIGH for two minutes.

Put the steak in the air fryer's basket. Turn on the air fryer after placing the basket inside. Cook for 6 to 8 minutes on each side at 400°F or until desired doneness. Take out of the basket, then stand it for five minutes. Slice the meat thinly, going against the grain;

Fold a tortilla over the steak, onion, and salsa. You could also serve it with lime and avocado wedges.

Nutritional value per serving: 311 calories, 11 grams of fat, 49 milligrams of cholesterol, 501 milligrams of sodium, 27 grams of carbohydrates, 2.8 grams of sugar, 4 grams of fiber, and 26 grams of protein (one fajita).

24. *Cooked Pork Chops*

Serving Size: 4

Preparation time: 15 minutes

Ingredients:

- Boneless Pork loin chops;

- Garlic powder, one teaspoon worth

- Paprika, one teaspoon

- A cup and a third of almond flour

- 1/4 cup of finely grated Parmesan cheese

- 1 teaspoon Creole seasoning

- Spray for frying

Directions:

Set your air fryer's temperature to 375 degrees Fahrenheit (190 degrees Celsius). Combine the almond flour, cheese, garlic powder, paprika, and Creole seasoning in a pie plate or other shallow dish.
Use the almond flour mixture to coat each pork chop, then place in the fridge.
Use cooking spray to thoroughly coat both sides of the pork chops and set them aside.
Position the meat in the air fryer basket in one continuous layer.
Bake the pork at 375 degrees Fahrenheit (190 degrees Celsius) for 6-7 minutes, flip it over, and bake it for an additional 6-7 minutes (the internal temperature should be 145 degrees Fahrenheit).

Nutritional value per serving: 1 pork chop contains 308 calories, 14 grams of fat, 91 milligrams of cholesterol, 311 milligrams of sodium, 4.2 grams of carbohydrates, 0 grams of sugar, 1 gram of fiber, and 37 grams of protein.

25.   *Turkey-based Croquettes*

Serving Size: 6

Preparation time: 25 minutes

Ingredients:

- 1 shallot, finely minced;

- Cooked turkey weighing three cups (finely chopped)

- 1-1/4 cups bread crumbs made from panko

- 2 cups of potatoes mashed (to which milk and butter have been added)

- A quarter-cup of grated Parmesan cheese

- 1/2 cup of Swiss cheese, shredded

- 1 tsp freshly minced sage

- 0.5 tsp. of salt

- 1/8 teaspoon pepper

- 2 teaspoons fresh rosemary, minced

- Cooking spray flavored like butter

- 1 egg

- Water, 2 tablespoons

- Sour milk

Directions:

Turn the air fryer on and preheat it to 350 degrees. The mashed potatoes, Parmesan cheese, Swiss cheese, shallot, rosemary, sage, salt, and pepper should all be combined in a sizable bowl. After adding the cooked turkey, combine everything. Combine the egg and the water in a bowl that is roughly the same size. Bread crumbs should be placed in a different bowl. The first mixture should be used to make 12 one-inch-thick turkey patties. The patties should then be covered in bread crumbs before being dipped in the egg mixture. Place the turkey patties in a single layer in the air fryer's basket and spray cooking spray with a buttery flavor on top of each ball.

Add more frying spray and turn the chicken over halfway through cooking for an additional 9 to 10 minutes, or until the chicken is browned.

Serve with sour cream and while still hot.

Nutritional value per serving: 319 calories, 19 grams of carbohydrates, 2 grams of sugars, 2 grams of fiber, 9 grams of fat, 130 milligrams of cholesterol, 669 milligrams of sodium, and 30 grams of protein.

26. *Chicken Breast*

Serving Size: 8

Preparation time: 2 hours and 45 minutes

Ingredients:

- A cup of water, two

- 2 teaspoons kosher salt

- 2 to 3 fresh herb sprigs (such as sage, rosemary, and thyme), as well as fresh herbs chopped for garnish

- 1 crushed garlic clove

- 2 boneless, skinless chicken breasts weighing 8 ounces

- 1/2 tsp. paprika

- 1/2 tsp. of onion powder

- 1/2 teaspoon ground pepper

Directions:

Mix the water, salt, herbs, and garlic in a medium bowl. Allow to rest for approximately 5 minutes, stirring once or twice, until the salt dissolves. Place the chicken in a shallow container with a lid or a carton sealable plastic bag after adding the brine to it. Place in the refrigerator for up to 12 hours with a cover or seal.

Clean out the chicken. Now dry it off and discard the liquid. On all sides of the chicken, paprika, onion powder, and pepper must be properly distributed, the air fryer to 375 degrees. Place the chicken in the fryer basket after liberally spraying it with heating oil. Cook for 7 minutes, or until one side is crisp. Cook the chicken for about 7 minutes, or until a thermometer inserted in the center registers 165°F, after spraying some cooking spray on it. Take five minutes to observe. Add chopped herbs as a garnish if preferred.

Nutritional value per serving: 369 calories, 27 grams of carbohydrates, 2 grams of sugars, 2 grams of fiber, 10 grams of fat, 400 milligrams of sodium, and 37 grams of protein.

27. *Pearl Tacos*

Serving Size: 4

Preparation time: 30 minutes

Ingredients:

- 2 cups finely chopped green cabbage
- 1/4 cup fresh cilantro, finely chopped
- 1 finely sliced scallion
- Divided 5 teaspoons of lime juice (from 2 limes)
- One big avocado
- 2 teaspoons sour cream
- 1 grated little garlic clove
- 1/4 cup salt
- One big egg white
- 1/3 cup whole-wheat dry breadcrumbs
- Mahi-mahi fillets weighing 1 pound, skinless, cut into 2- to 3-inch strips
- Avocado oil spray for cooking
- 8 warmed, six-inch corn tortillas
- 1 chopped medium tomato
- Serving wedges of lime

Directions:

Mix the cabbage, cilantro, scallion, 2 tsp lime juice, and avocado oil in a medium bowl. Place aside. Avocados must be split in half lengthwise, and the pulp must be transferred with a spoon into the container of a small food processor. The remaining three tablespoons of lime juice, sour cream, salt, and garlic should all be smooth after about 30 seconds of processing. (Alternatively, mash the mixture with a fork until it has the desired consistency.) Set aside.

400 degrees Fahrenheit should be reached when an air fryer is heated. In such a shallow dish, add the egg white and whisk until foamy. Put breadcrumbs and chili powder in another shallow dish. Dry the fish with a paper towel. Put the fish in the breadcrumb mixture now, coating it thoroughly. Apply egg white to the fish, letting extra drip off. If necessary, work in batches as you arrange the fish in an even layer in the fryer basket. Apply frying spray liberally to the fish. 3 minutes should be enough to get one side crispy and browned. 3 minutes after folding, cook the salmon until it is crisp and flakes easily. Fish must be cut into pieces by the claws.

Nutritional value per serving: 101 calories, 3 grams of protein, 10 grams of carbohydrates, 2.8 grams of fiber, 7.7 grams of sugars, 5 grams of fat, 7 milligrams of cholesterol, and 317 milligrams of sodium.

28. *Frittata With Cheddar And Zucchini*

Serving Size: 4

Preparation time: 30 minutes

Ingredients:

- 4 eggs or 1 cup of thawed, refrigerated, or frozen egg product

- 1/2 cup of reduced-fat, coarsely shredded cheddar cheese

- 2 teaspoons freshly chopped flat-leaf parsley

- 1/4 teaspoon ground pepper

- 1/8 tsp. salt

- Olive oil, 2 tablespoons

- ounces of sliced and lengthwise halved zucchini

- Sliced green onions, four

Directions:

A rack should be placed in the upper third of the oven, and it should be preheated to 450 degrees F. Whisk together the eggs, cheese, pepper, salt, and 1/2 the parsley in a medium bowl. Place aside. Warm up the olive oil in a 9- to 10-inch ovenproof skillet over medium-high heat. Add the zucchini and inexperienced onions; cook, stirring regularly, for 5 to 8 minutes, or until soft. Pour the egg mixture over the vegetables with caution. heat to a medium setting. Run a spatula around the edge of the skillet as the mixture sets, raising the egg mixture so that the liquid component flows below. Cook and lift edges for a further five minutes, or until the egg mixture is almost set (the floor will be moist). Reduce heat as much as necessary to prevent over-browning.
Inside the oven, put the skillet. Bake the frittata for about 5 minutes, or until it is arranged and the top is golden. Add the final 2 teaspoons of parsley. wedges should be cut. Serve hot.

Nutritional value per serving: 115 calories, 6 carbs, 8 grams of protein, 7 grams of fat, 400 milligrams of sodium, 1 gram of fiber, and 3 grams of sugar.

29.   Salmon With Pepper And Lemon

Serving Size: 4

Preparation time: 15 minutes

Ingredients:

• 4 skin-on salmon fillets, ideally wild Alaskan, weighing 5 to 6 ounces.

• 1 tablespoon black pepper, cracked

• 1/2 tsp. paprika

• 1/2 tsp. of garlic powder

• 1/2 tsp. salt

• 1 tablespoon lemon zest, grated

• 2 teaspoons divided lemon juice

• 2 teaspoons freshly chopped parsley.

• A pinch of salty seaweed

Directions:

Place the salmon in a medium basin, pores and skin-facet down. Pat dry. Add pepper, paprika, garlic powder, salt, and 1 teaspoon of lemon juice.
In a large nonstick pan, heat the oil over medium-high heat until it shimmers. Add the salmon, skin side down, and cook for four minutes, or until the rims are opaque and the skin and pores easily release from the pan. Turn the salmon while lowering the heat. Cook the salmon for another three to five minutes, or until an instant-read thermometer inserted within the thickest portion of the fish reads 145°F. The final teaspoon of lemon juice, lemon zest, parsley, and flaky salt should be sprinkled over the salmon.

Nutritional value per serving: 340 calories, 27 grams of carbohydrates, 7 grams of sugars, 12 grams of fiber, 10 grams of fat, 200 milligrams of sodium, and 37 grams of protein.

30. *Rosemary Chicken*

Serving Size: 4

Preparation time: 35 minutes

Ingredients:

• 4 tablespoons olive or canola oil

• 3 minced garlic cloves

• 1/4 cup of kosher salt

• 1/2 tsp. freshly chopped rosemary

• 1 1/2 tablespoons freshly ground black pepper

• 1 package (20 ounces) of chilled sweet potatoes chopped, such as Simply Potatoes

• 2 (8-ounce) chicken breast halves, cut in half crosswise.

• 1 finely sliced lemon

Directions:

Warm up 3 Tbsps of the oil in a 12-inch nonstick skillet over medium heat. Add the garlic, 1/4 cup of rosemary, 1/2 cup of salt, and 1/4 cup of pepper. Potatoes are added; toss to coat. 5 minutes of covered cooking (do not stir). Potatoes should be pushed to at least one edge of the skillet. To a different area of the skillet, add the last tablespoon of oil. Place the chicken and potatoes in the skillet. Cook for eight minutes uncovered.
Stir the potatoes and turn the chicken. Add the remaining 1/4 tsp of salt, rosemary, and pepper to the chicken. Add lemon slices on top. Cook, covered, for an additional 8 to 10 minutes, or until the chicken is done (165 degrees F), and the potatoes are brown. (If necessary, remove potatoes as they are finished cooking and continue to simmer chicken until done.) Added rosemary can be sprinkled on top, if desired.

Nutritional value per serving: 438 calories, 31 grams of protein, 32 grams of fat, 158 milligrams of cholesterol, and 268 milligrams of sodium in addition to other nutrients.

Dinner

1. Avocado Hummus

Serving Size: 10

Preparation time: 10 minutes

Ingredients:

- 1 (15-ounce) can of chickpeas with no additional salt

- One ripe avocado, pitted and cut in half.

- 1 cup fresh leaves of cilantro

- 1/4 tahini cup

- Extra virgin olive oil, 1/4 cup

- Lemon juice, 1/4 cup

- One garlic clove

- 1 teaspoon cumin powder

- 1/2 tsp. salt

Directions:

2 tablespoons of the chickpea liquid should be saved aside after draining. To a food processor, add the chickpeas and the liquid you saved. You should also include avocado, cilantro, tahini, oil, lemon juice, garlic, cumin, and salt. Blend until extremely smooth. Serve with veggie chips, pita chips, or assorted crudités.

Nutritional value per serving: 101 calories, 3 grams of protein, 10 grams of carbohydrates, 2.8 grams of fiber, 7.7 grams of sugars, 5 grams of fat, 7 milligrams of cholesterol, and 317 milligrams of sodium.

2. *Verde Chicken Chili*

Serving Size: 6

Preparation time: 30 minutes

Ingredients:

- 2 (15 ounce) cans of rinsed, split, no-salt-added pinto beans

- Canola oil, 1 teaspoon

- 1 12 pounds of trimmed, diced chicken thighs that are boneless and skinless.

- 2 cups of yellow onion, chopped (1 medium)

- 2 cups of poblano peppers, chopped (2 large)

- 1 1/2 teaspoons (or 5 chopped garlic cloves)

- 4 cups of chicken stock without salt

- 1 1/2 cups of salted green salsa

- 1/2 tsp. salt

- 2 cups of corn kernels, frozen (about 12 ounces)

- 2 cups of spinach, chopped (about 2 ounces)

- 1 1/2 cups of fresh cilantro, roughly chopped

- 6 teaspoons sour cream

Directions:

Use a whisk or potato masher to thoroughly mash 1 cup of beans in a small bowl. The oil should be heated over high heat in a big, sturdy saucepan. When the chicken is browned, add it and cook for 4 to 5 minutes while stirring occasionally. Poblanos, onion, and garlic should be added. Cook the onion for 4 to 5 minutes, or until it is translucent and tender.

Add the remaining whole beans, mashed beans, salsa, salt, and stock. boiling point. Once the chicken is thoroughly cooked, lower the heat to medium and let it simmer for about 3 minutes. Mix in with cilantro, spinach, and corn. Cook the spinach for about a minute, or until it wilts. Top with sour cream before serving.

Nutritional value per serving: 33 grams of carbohydrates, 2.8 grams of sugars, 1 gram of fiber, 10 grams of fat, 87 milligrams of cholesterol, 499 milligrams of sodium, and 24 grams of protein in this dish.

3. *Spinach And Roasted Sweet Potatoes*

Serving Size: 4

Preparation time: 40 minutes

Ingredients:

• Divided 5 teaspoons of extra virgin olive oil

• Divided 1/2 tsp of ground pepper

• Divided 1/4 tsp of salt

• 1/2 cup of fresh basil leaves packed

• 3 teaspoons of cider vinegar

• 1 teaspoon of finely minced shallot

• 2 tablespoons of whole-grain mustard

• Ten cups of young spinach

• 1 (15-ounce) can of washed low-sodium cannellini beans

• 2 cups of finely minced cabbage

• 1 cup of red bell pepper, chopped

• 1/3 cup toasty pecans, chopped

Directions:

Set the oven to 425°F. Sweet potatoes, 1 tablespoon oil, 1/4 cup pepper, and 1/8 cup salt should all be combined in a large basin. Roast for 15 to 18 minutes, stirring once, on a big rimmed baking sheet. Give it at least 10 minutes to cool.

Add the basil to the mini food processor along with the remaining 1/4 cup oil, vinegar, shallot, mustard, and the final 1/4 teaspoon each of pepper and salt while everything else is going on. until a procedure that was mostly fluid. Put inside the large basin. Add the spinach, beans, cabbage, bell pepper, pecans, and sweet potatoes that have been chilled. Toss to coat.

Nutritional value per serving: 311 calories, 11 grams of fat, 49 milligrams of cholesterol, 501 milligrams of sodium, 27 grams of carbohydrates, 2.8 grams of sugar, 4 grams of fiber, and 26 grams of protein (one fajita).

4. Sandwich With Chicken And Tomatoes

Serving Size: 1

Preparation time: 10 minutes

Ingredients:

• Two slices of whole-grain bread

• A ripe avocado, 1/4

• 3 ounces cooked, sliced boneless, skinless chicken breast

Directions:

Heat the oven to 425°F. Oil should be heated over medium-high heat in a big cast-iron skillet. Sweet potatoes with 1/4 tsp. salt. Stirring occasionally, cook for 5 to 7 minutes or until beginning to brown. Depending on how soft they are, bake the sweet potatoes in the pan for 15 to 20 minutes. In a small bowl, combine the sour cream, lime juice, and the last grain of salt. Corn, beans, and cheese should be added to the sweet potatoes. The cheese needs to melt in the oven for an additional 5 minutes or so. As a garnish, include avocado, tomatoes, and scallions. Drizzle a sour cream mixture over top. Serve garnished with cilantro (if using).

5. Radishes

Serving Size: 6   **Prep time:** 10 minutes

Ingredients:

• 2-1/4 pounds radishes (trimmed and quartered)

• 1 tablespoon minced fresh oregano

• 1/4 teaspoon salt

• 1/8 teaspoon pepper

Directions:

Toss radishes with oil, oregano, salt, and pepper. Place radishes in a single layer in your air fryer basket. Optional: Sprinkle with 1/4 teaspoon red pepper flakes. Cook at 375° for 15 minutes or until tender.

Nutritional value per serving (2/3 cup): 86 Calories, 5.8g Carbohydrates, 2.9g Sugars, 3g Fiber, 6g Fat, 159mg Sodium, 1g Protein.

6. *Vegetables-Made Omelet*

Serving Size: 4

Preparation time: 30 minutes

Ingredients:

- 12 cup well-drained, no-salt-added diced tomatoes with basil, garlic, and oregano

- 1/2 cup seeded and sliced cucumber

- 1/2 cup sliced summer yellow squash

- A pitted, peeled, and sliced half an avocado

- 2 eggs

- 1 cup thawed, chilled or frozen egg product

- Water, 2 teaspoons

- 1 tablespoon crumbled dried basil

- 1/4 cup salt

- 1/4 teaspoon ground pepper

- Cooking oil nonstick

- 1/4 cup of shredded low-fat Monterey Jack cheese with jalapenos

- 1 freshly chopped chives

Directions:

Combine tomatoes, cucumber, squash, and avocado in a medium bowl to create the filling. Place aside. Combine the eggs, egg product, water, basil, salt, and pepper in a medium bowl.

Cooking spray should be liberally applied to an 8-inch nonstick skillet for each omelet. Over medium heat, warm the skillet. A generous 1/3 cup of the egg mixture should be added to the hot skillet. Begin immediately by whisking eggs slowly but consistently with a wooden spatula until the mixture resembles cooked egg parts encircled by liquid egg. Give up stirring. Cook the egg for a further 30 to 60 seconds, or until it is just barely glossy. Over one omelet side, spoon half a cup of the filling. Omelet should be carefully folded over filling. With extreme caution, remove the omelet from the skillet. Make four omelets altogether by repeating the process, wiping the skillet clean with paper towels, and distributing cooking spray between the omelets. Each omelet should have 1 Tsp of cheese on top. Add chives as a garnish if preferred.

Nutritional value per serving: 16 grams of carbohydrates, 8 grams of sugar, 14 grams of protein, and 7.3 grams of fat in this dish.

7. *Baked Shrimps And Cauliflower*

Serving Size: 6

Preparation time: 55 minutes

Ingredients:

• 4 cups of tiny florets of cauliflower (1 medium head)

• 1/2 cup minced onion

•Olive oil, 2 teaspoons

• 1/2 tsp. red pepper flakes

• 1/4 cup salt

• 1 pound of medium-sized, peeled, deveined shrimp, either fresh or frozen (thawed).

• 2 (14.5 ounce) cans of drained, no-salt-added diced tomatoes

• 2 minced garlic cloves

• One teaspoon lemon zest

• 1/2 cup of reduced-fat feta cheese crumbles

• 1 teaspoon freshly sliced dill

• 4 slices of lemon

Directions:

Heat the oven to 425 degrees. Cauliflower, onion, oil, salt, and crushed red pepper should all be combined in a big bowl. The ingredients should be distributed in a little, shallow metal roasting pan. The cauliflower should only be tender after 25 minutes of baking.

The shrimp should be rinsed and dried by patting. In a medium bowl, mix the shrimp, tomatoes, garlic, and lemon zest. Pour the shrimp mixture on top of the cauliflower mixture. The shrimp should bake for an additional 15 minutes or until opaque. After combining cheese and dill, sprinkle over shrimp mixture. If desired, garnish with lemon slices.

Nutritional value per serving: 109 calories, 3.9 grams of fat, 148 milligrams of sodium, 16 grams of carbohydrates, 1 gram of sugar, 2 grams of fiber, and 2 grams of protein in a single serving (one cup).

8. Wraps Of Scallops And Bacon

Serving Size: 6

Preparation time: 10 minutes

Ingredients:

- One quarter-teaspoon of paprika and three thin pieces of bacon with the center cut off.

- Extra-virgin olive oil, 1 teaspoon

- 1/4 teaspoon of black pepper, crushed

- One-half a medium sea scallop

Directions:

With paper towels, pat the scallops dry. The side muscle of each scallop must be removed and discarded. Create twelve separate strips of bacon by halving each piece of bacon lengthwise and then cutting it across. Each scallop has to have one piece of bacon wrapped around it, with the ends of the strips slightly overlapping.

Place a wooden pick through the opposite side of the scallop and both ends of the bacon to keep the bacon in place. With the aid of a small oil brush, evenly distribute the pepper and paprika over the scallops. Place the scallops in the basket of your air fryer and cook them for 10 to 12 minutes at 375 degrees Fahrenheit.

Nutritional value per serving: 9 milligrams of cholesterol, 181 milligrams of sodium, 4.7 grams of protein, 1 gram of carbs, 2 grams of fat, and 41 calories.

9. Tenders Of Chicken

Serving Size: 4

Preparation time: 15 minutes

Ingredients:

- Chicken tenders weighing 1 pound;

- 1 cup of panko breadcrumbs made from whole wheat;

- 2 eggs

- 2 teaspoons of seasoning mix;

- Whole-wheat flour, 1/4 cup;

- a half-teaspoon of salt

- 1/4 teaspoon of pepper, ground;

- cooking spray; serving-related honey mustard

Directions:

Dry the chicken tenders completely with a paper towel. Toss breadcrumbs with 2 teaspoons of Italian seasoning, salt, pepper, and a pinch of black pepper on a dish.

Transfer the beaten eggs to a sizable, long, rectangular dish and mix them together. Move the flour to a second, separate, broad, shallow dish and whisk it until it's thoroughly combined. Increase the air fryer's internal temperature to 400 degrees.

Before dipping the chicken tenders in the egg mixture, dust them with flour on both sides. Place the breaded chicken into the breadcrumb mixture, coating both sides, and pressing the crumbs into the chicken. Apply a small layer of nonstick cooking spray to a baking sheet. Place breaded chicken tenders in the air fryer basket and bake for 8 to 10 minutes, or until golden and thoroughly cooked through (the internal temperature should be 165 degrees Fahrenheit). Season with honey mustard before serving.

Nutritional value per serving: 228 calories, 29 grams of protein, 13 grams of carbs, 2 grams of fiber, 1 gram of sugar, 4 grams of fat, 161 milligrams of cholesterol, and 451 milligrams of sodium.

10. *Meatballs*

Serving Size: 8

Preparation time: 25 minutes

Ingredients:

- 3 tsp. whole-wheat panko breadcrumbs
- One big egg
- 90 percent lean ground beef, 1 lb.
- One little red onion (grated)
- One-fourth cup Parmesan cheese (grated)
- 1 teaspoon of seasoning mix

- 1/4 tsp. powdered onion
- 1/2 teaspoon of powdered garlic
- 0.4 teaspoon freshly ground pepper
- Spray for frying
- Serving marinara sauce
- Frying cooking spray

Directions:

Cooking spray the air fryer basket and preheat the air fryer to 370 degrees Fahrenheit. Fill the air fryer with the food. Combine all the ingredients, excluding the marinara sauce and cooking spray, in a bowl.

Using flour-dusted hands, form the dough into 16 identically sized balls. Before arranging the meatballs in a single layer in the basket of your air fryer, spray them with oil. Put in the oven and bake for 8 minutes, or until the center is 165 degrees Fahrenheit and the outside is golden brown.

Serve hot with marinara sauce on the side.

Nutritional value per serving: 121 calories, 12 grams of protein, 2.8 grams of carbs, 1 gram of sugar, 5 grams of fat, 59 milligrams of cholesterol, and 311 milligrams of sodium.

11.   *Chicken Drumsticks*

Serving Size: 6

Preparation time: 40 minutes

Ingredients:

- Six drumsticks of chicken

- 1/4 teaspoon powdered garlic

- Two tablespoons of curry powder

- 1/4 tsp. cumin

- 1/4 tsp. salt

- 3 tablespoons of unflavored Greek yogurt

- Juiced half a lemon

- 1/4 tsp. pepper

Directions:

In a small bowl, combine the cumin, curry powder, salt, pepper, and garlic powder. Make sure it is properly blended by mixing. Combine the chicken drumsticks, Greek yogurt, spice mixture, and lemon juice in a zip-top bag. Seal the bag and give it a light shake. To make sure the chicken is well coated, you can move it around with your hand.

Marinate the bag for no longer than 30 minutes in the refrigerator.

Take the chicken drumsticks out of the bag and place them in the basket of the air dryer. Fry the drumsticks in the air for 10 minutes at 400 degrees Fahrenheit. After flipping the drumsticks, cook them for an additional 15 minutes.

Nutritional value per serving: 170 calories, 21g of protein, 1g of carbohydrate, 7g of fat, and 179mg of salt.

12.   *Chicken Nuggets with Sweet Potatoes*

Serving Size: 24

Preparation time: 20 minutes

Ingredients:

- 1 lb. of chicken ground

- A teaspoon of onion powder

- A single sweet potato

- Two cups of whole-wheat crackers

- A quarter cup oat flour

- 1/8 teaspoon of garlic powder

- Optional: 1/2 teaspoon salt

Directions:

Create a coarse flour from the crackers. In a bowl, set aside. Cut the sweet potato into dice.

Combine the oat flour, ground chicken, and seasoning with the sweet potato dice. For these three stages, a food processor can be used. Use the mixture to coat the crushed crackers. Make sure the coating is thick.

Use paper to line the air fryer tray. Set the air fryer's temperature to 360°F.

Use avocado oil to sparingly coat the air fryer tray to avoid sticking. Place the coated chicken nuggets in the tray and drizzle extra avocado oil over the top. Prepare the food for 16 minutes.

Nutritional value per serving: 88 calories, 9g of carbohydrates, 1g of fiber, 2g of sugar, 4.2g of protein, 2.8g of fat, 15mg of cholesterol, and 140mg of sodium make up the meal.

13. *Teriyaki Air Fryer for Salmon*

Serving Size: 4

Preparation time: 10 minutes

Ingredients:

Because of the teriyaki sauce

- 1/8 cup mirin (sweetened sake)
- 1/2 cup soy sauce low in sodium
- Two garlic cloves (minced)

- Brown sugar, 2 teaspoons
- A quarter-teaspoon of toasted sesame oil
- One-inch gingerbread (minced)

Salmon

- 1 1/2 pounds of skin-on salmon filets (cut into 4 equal sized pieces)

Directions:

Place the prepared teriyaki sauce ingredients in a small saucepan and heat to a boil over medium-high heat. Remove from burner after 5 minutes of simmering. Put the salmon and 3/4 of the sauce in a zip-top bag that can be sealed. Spend 30 minutes relaxing at room temperature.

Spray cooking spray within the frying chamber, on the bottom and top racks, and all over the air fryer to prepare it. Set the air fryer's temperature to 390°F. Salmon should be cooked in the air fryer for 6 minutes, at a temperature of 145°F, after being removed from the marinade.

Take out of the air fryer and top with a lime slice and sesame seeds. Use the leftover teriyaki sauce to serve. Enjoy!

Nutritional value per serving: 298 calories, 13g of carbohydrates Protein: 31g, Sugar: 9g, Fat: 12g, Cholesterol: 89mg, Sodium: 1248mg, Fiber: 1g.

14.   *Shrimp Air-Fried*

Serving Size: 4

Preparation time: 10 minutes

Ingredients:

- 1 teaspoon lemon juice.

- 1 tablespoon melted unsalted butter

- 1 tsp. of garlic (minced)

- 1 lb. of raw, big shrimp (peeled and deveined)

- Add pepper and salt to taste (optional)

- Minced parsley (to garnish)

Directions:

4 minutes of 350°F air fryer preheat. In a sizable bowl, combine the shrimp, butter, garlic, salt, pepper, and lemon juice.

In the air fryer, add the shrimp mixture and cook for at least 8 minutes. Add lemon wedges and parsley to garnish.

Serve hot.

Nutritional value per serving: 110 calories, 1 g of carbohydrates, 0 g of fiber, 0 g of sugar, 3.8 g of fat, 148 mg of cholesterol, 721 mg of sodium, and 18 g of protein.

15. *Fajitas With Chicken*

Serving Size: 4

Preparation time: 15 minutes

Ingredients:

- One pound of skinless, boneless chicken breast

- One sizable red onion (thinly sliced)

- 8 warmed tortillas (your favorite).

- 1/4 cup fresh coriander (chopped)

- Olive oil, 1 tablespoon

- 1 tbsp fajita seasoning

- 1 tbsp lime juice

- 2 bell peppers (seeded and thinly sliced) (seeded and thinly sliced)

- Desired toppings

Directions:

Make thin strips out of the chicken. Combine the strips with the fajita seasoning, olive oil, onion, and bell pepper in a bowl. To enable coating, gently shake the dish or stir.

Allow to chill for at least 30 minutes or up to 5 hours. Set the air fryer's temperature to 390 degrees Fahrenheit for around 5 minutes. When the chicken is fully cooked and the vegetables are soft, air-fry the chicken mixture for about 15 minutes.

Combine the cooked chicken, cilantro, jalapeño, lime juice, and in a bowl. Present with the tortillas and toppings of your choosing.

Nutritional value per serving: 237 calories, 4.8 grams of carbs, 1 gram of fiber, 2.1 grams of sugar, 7 grams of fat, 101 mg of cholesterol, 235 mg of sodium, and 32 grams of protein.

16. *Weight Loss Soup*

Serving Size: 8

Preparation time: 1 hour

Ingredients:

- Two tablespoons of virgin olive oil

- 1 chopped medium onion

- Chopped 2 medium carrots

- 2 celery stalks, chopped

- 12 ounces freshly chopped 1/2-inch green beans

- 2 minced garlic cloves

- 8 cups of low-sodium vegetable broth or chicken broth with no salt added

- 2 washed, low-sodium (15 ounce) cans of cannellini beans

- Four cups of kale, chopped

- 2 chopped medium zucchini

- Four seeded and sliced Roma tomatoes

- 2 tablespoons of red wine vinegar

- 1/4 cup salt

- 1/2 teaspoon ground pepper

- 8 tablespoons made-up pesto

Directions:

Medium-high heat is used to warm the oil in a large saucepan. Green beans, onion, carrot, celery, and garlic should all be added. Cook the vegetables, stirring frequently, for about 10 minutes, or until they begin to soften.

Step 2's addition of the broth is followed by a boil. Reduce the heat to a simmer for 10 minutes while tossing the vegetables occasionally. Add tomatoes, vinegar, salt, pepper, white beans, kale, and zucchini. Turn increase the heat and continue to simmer for about 10 minutes, or until the kale and zucchini are soft.

Each soup bowl should have a spoonful of pesto on top.

Nutritional value per serving: 9 milligrams of cholesterol, 181 milligrams of sodium, 4.7 grams of protein, 1 gram of carbs, 2 grams of fat, and 41 calories.

17.   *Salmon Stuffed Avocadoes*

Serving Size: 4

Preparation time: 15 minutes

Ingredients:

- 1/2 cup plain nonfat Greek yogurt
- 1/2 cup celery, chopped
- 2 tsp freshly chopped parsley
- 2 tablespoons mayo
- 1 teaspoon of Dijon mustard

- 1/8 tsp. salt
- 1/8 teaspoon ground pepper
- 2 cans of salmon, each weighing 5 ounces, drained, flaked, and boneless
- Two avos
- Minced chives as a garnish

Directions:

Mix the yogurt, celery, parsley, lime juice, mayonnaise, mustard, salt, and pepper in a medium bowl. Fish has been well mixed in. Avocados should be pitted and divided lengthwise. One tablespoon of the flesh from each avocado, cut in half, should be placed in a small bowl. Removed avocado flesh should be mashed with a fork and combined with the salmon mixture.

Place a heap of the salmon mixture, equal to about 14 cup, on top of each avocado half. Add chives as a garnish if preferred.

Nutritional value per serving: 170 calories, 21g of protein, 1g of carbohydrate, 7g of fat, and 179mg of salt.

18.   *Tomato Soup*

Serving Size: 4

Preparation time: 30 minutes

Ingredients:

- 2 pounds of seeded and cored tomatoes (see Tip)

- One and a half cups of finely chopped red sweet peppers

- 1 cup of low-sodium chicken or veggie broth

- 1/4 cup finely sliced sweet onion

- 1/4 cup freshly chopped basil

- 2 teaspoons thick cream

- 1 tsp. of honey

- 1 croutons with grilled cheese

Directions:

Small batches of tomatoes, peppers, broth, onion, and basil should be blended or processed together. Blend or process until the covered surface is smooth. Put all of the blended mixture in a large pot. Cook on medium for 5 to 6 minutes, or until well cooked. Stir in the cream and honey. If you'd like, garnish the servings with Grilled Cheese Croutons and additional basil. Serve warm.

Nutritional value per serving: 88 calories, 9g of carbohydrates, 1g of fiber, 2g of sugar, 4.2g of protein, 2.8g of fat, 15mg of cholesterol, and 140mg of sodium make up the meal.

19.   *Roasted Carrots Soup*

Serving Size: 4

Preparation time: 1 hour, 10 minutes

Ingredients:

- 1 1/2 pounds of peeled and sliced, 2- to 3-inch carrots

- 1 onion, quartered and peeled

- 3 garlic cloves, unpeeled

- 1 (1 inch) piece of freshly peeled and sliced ginger

- Olive oil, 1 teaspoon

- 2 cups of almond milk without sugar

- 1 cup of chicken broth low in salt

- 1 teaspoon of black pepper, coarsely ground

- 1 cup of water

- 1 tablespoon grated carrot

- 1 leaves of fresh basil

Directions:

Set the oven to 400 degrees Fahrenheit. Combine the chopped carrots with the onion, garlic, and ginger in a big basin. Add some olive oil and stir to coat. On a baking pan measuring 15x10x1 inches, arrange the greens in a single layer. Bake for 50 to 60 minutes, or until very soft. Cool a little. Garlic cloves should be squeezed out of their skins and placed in a food processor or blender. Add the roasted carrots, onion, and ginger; cover the mixture or system and turn it on and off again until the greens are chopped. Add pepper, broth, and almond milk. Systematize or combine until smooth. To a medium saucepan, transfer. The water is stirred. Cook and stir until thoroughly cooked. Basil leaves and carrot shavings can be used as garnish, if preferred.

Nutritional value per serving: 88 calories, 9g of carbohydrates, 1g of fiber, 2g of sugar, 4.2g of protein, 2.8g of fat, 15mg of cholesterol, and 140mg of sodium make up the meal.

20. *Chicken Bowl*

Serving Size: 4

Preparation time: 30 minutes

Ingredients:

- 1 serving of cooked quinoa

- 1 serving of cooked brown rice

- Cooked Chili-Lime Chicken, 1 pound
(see Associated recipe)

- 1 cup of thinly sliced jicama

- 1 cup thawed frozen corn

- 1 serving of pico de gallo

- 1 diced avocado

- 1/2 cup freshly chopped cilantro

- Slices of lime

- Spicy condiments like Cholula

Directions:

After combining the two grains, divide the mixture among the four single-serving containers with lids. Distribute the chicken, jicama, corn, avocado, cilantro, pico de gallo, and evenly. Seal the containers and keep them cold for up to 4 days. Serve with lime wedges and a hot sauce.

Nutritional value per serving: 120 calories, 6g of carbohydrates, 1g of fiber, 2g of sugar, 8g of protein, 2g of fat, 20mg of cholesterol, and 112mg of sodium.

21.   *Baked Banana Nut*

Serving Size: 12

Preparation time: 50 minutes

Ingredients:

- Three cups of rolled oats (see Tip)

- 1 1/2 cups of nonfat milk

- 2 mashed, ripe bananas (approximately 3/4 cup)

- 1/3 cup brown sugar in a bag

- 2 big, lightly beaten eggs

- 1 tablespoon baking soda

- 1 teaspoon cinnamon powder

- A teaspoon of vanilla extract

- 1/2 tsp. salt

- 1/2 cup chopped, toasted pecans

Directions:

Set the oven to 375°F. In a muffin pan, mist frying oil. Combine the oats, milk, bananas, brown sugar, eggs, baking powder, cinnamon, vanilla, and salt in a large basin. Fold in pecans. Each muffin cup should have about 1/3 cup of mixture in it. 25 minutes should be allotted for baking, or until a toothpick inserted in the center comes out clean. Remove the pan and set it on a wire rack after allowing it to cool for ten minutes. Serve warm or at room temperature.

Nutritional value per serving: 237 calories, 4.8 grams of carbs, 1 gram of fiber, 2.1 grams of sugar, 7 grams of fat, 101 mg of cholesterol, 235 mg of sodium, and 32 grams of protein.

22.   *Winter Kale And Quinoa Salad*

Serving Size: 2

Preparation time: 35 minutes

Ingredients:

- 1 small sweet potato, peeled, and chopped into pieces measuring 1/2 cup

- Divided 2 12 Tbsps of olive oil

- 1/2 avocado

- 1 teaspoon lime juice

- 1 peeled garlic clove

- 1/2 tsp. cumin powder

- 1/8 tsp. salt

- 1/8 teaspoon ground pepper

- 1-2 Tbsp. of water

- 1 serving of cooked quinoa (see Associated Recipes)

- 1/4 cup washed, no-salt-added, canned black beans

- 1.25 cups of finely chopped baby kale

- Pepitas, 2 tsp

- A sliced scallion, one

Directions:

Set the oven to 400 degrees Fahrenheit. Put sweet potatoes and 1 teaspoon oil on a large baking sheet with a rim. Roast for about 25 minutes, stirring as soon as the halfway mark.

In the meantime, combine the remaining 12 tsp. oil, avocado, lime juice, garlic, cumin, salt, and pepper in a food processor or blender. Blend or process until smooth. If necessary, add 1 Tbsp. of water to reach the desired consistency. In a medium bowl, mix the kale, black beans, quinoa, and candied potatoes. Add the avocado dressing and toss to coat after a light drizzle. Add pepitas and scallion on top.

Nutritional value per serving: 109 calories, 3.9 grams of fat, 148 milligrams of sodium, 16 grams of carbohydrates, 1 gram of sugar, 2 grams of fiber, and 2 grams of protein in a single serving (one cup).

23.   *Sesame Noodles With Chicken*

Serving Size: 4

Preparation time: 20 minutes

Ingredients:

- Eight ounces of whole wheat spaghetti

- 3 tablespoons dark, roasted sesame oil

- Chopped scallions, two

- Garlic, minced, 1 teaspoon

- 2 tablespoons fresh ginger, minced

- Brown sugar, 1 tablespoon

- 2 teaspoons of low-sodium soy sauce

- Two tablespoons of ketchup

- 8 ounces of cooked, shredded, skinless chicken breast

- 1 cup sliced carrots

- Snap peas, cut, one cup

- 3 tablespoons of toast sesame seeds

Directions:

According to the instructions on the package, cook spaghetti in a pot of boiling water. Drain, rinse, and then transfer to a sizable bowl. In a small saucepan, combine the sesame oil, scallions, garlic, ginger, and brown sugar. Heat till sizzling on a medium heat setting. For 15 seconds, cook. Ketchup and soy sauce are added after being taken out of the heat. Add the chicken, carrots, snap peas, sesame seeds, and mix well with the noodles.

Nutritional value per serving: 311 calories, 11 grams of fat, 49 milligrams of cholesterol, 501 milligrams of sodium, 27 grams of carbohydrates, 2.8 grams of sugar, 4 grams of fiber, and 26 grams of proteins.

24. *Mushroom's Shepherd Pie With Chicken*

Serving Size: 6

Preparation time: 1 hour, 25 minutes

Ingredients:

• 2 pounds Yukon Gold potatoes, cut into 1-inch slices and optionally peeled

• 1/2 cup of nonfat milk

• Two tablespoons of virgin olive oil

• 1/2 tsp. salt

• Two tablespoons of virgin olive oil

• 8 ounces of sliced and halved cremini (baby Bella) mushrooms

• A cup of onion, chopped

• 1/4 tsp dried thyme or 1 tbsp finely chopped fresh

• Divided 1/2 tsp of salt

• Half a cup dry sherry (see Tip)

• 1 1/2 cups of homemade chicken stock or low-sodium chicken broth

• 3 teaspoons of regular flour

• 2 cups of cooked chicken in half-inch cubes, or 10 ounces

Directions:

In a large saucepan, add potatoes and enough bloodless water to cover the potatoes by 2 inches. Dinner should be cooked for 12 to 14 minutes, until it is soft. Bring to a boil. Drain the potatoes, then add them back to the pan. Mash in milk, 2 teaspoons of oil, and 14 teaspoon of salt. Set the oven at 400 F. Spray cooking spray in an 8-inch rectangle pan or a similar 2-quart baking dish. To assemble the filling: In a large nonstick skillet, heat the oil over medium-high heat. Add the mushrooms, onion, thyme, and 1/four teaspoon of salt. Cook the meal, stirring regularly, for seven to nine minutes, or until the mushrooms start to brown. Add the sherry and whisk while preparing the meal for 1 to 2 minutes, or until virtually evaporated. In a bowl, combine flour and broth (or stock). Stirring for one to two minutes will cause the mixture to thicken after being added to the pan. Add the remaining 1/4 tsp salt and pepper, along with the chicken, peas, and carrots, and stir-fry for one minute. On top, spread the mashed potatoes. On a baking sheet, put the baking dish. Bake for 30 to 35 minutes, or until the potatoes are slightly browned and the mixture is bubbling.

Nutritional value per serving: 109 calories, 3.9 grams of fat, 148 milligrams of sodium, 16 grams of carbohydrates, 1 gram of sugar, 2 grams of fiber, and 2 grams of protein in a single serving (one cup).

25.   *Baked Chicken And Spaghetti Squash*

Serving Size: 8

Preparation time: 1 hour, 40 minutes

Ingredients:

• A single medium spaghetti squash (about 3 lbs.)

• 4 cups of florets from broccoli

• Canola oil, 1 teaspoon

• 1 package (10 ounces) of sliced mushrooms

• 1 medium onion, chopped finely

• 2 minced garlic cloves

• 1/2 teaspoon dried thyme

• 1/2 teaspoon ground pepper

• 2 (10-ounce) cans of cream of mushroom soup

with reduced sodium, such as Campbell's 25% Less Sodium

• 1 1/2 pounds of skinless, boneless chicken breasts, diced into small pieces.

• 1/2 cup extra-sharp Cheddar cheese, shredded

Directions:

Set oven to 375 degrees Fahrenheit. Apply cooking spray to eight-inch, rectangular baking dishes. Cut the squash in half lengthwise, then remove the seeds. Add 2 Tbsp. and place cut-side down in a microwave-safe dish. water. Cook in the microwave, uncovered, on High for 10 to 12 minutes, or until the flesh can be scraped with a fork but is still smooth and crisp. Put the strands on a dish and separate them. In the same microwave-safe dish, add 1 Tbsp. and the broccoli. cover and water. 2 to 3 minutes on High, stirring regularly, until just almost smooth-crisp. Drain, then set aside to cool. In the meantime, heat oil in a large nonstick skillet over medium-high heat. Add the mushrooms and simmer, stirring, for about eight minutes, or until their juices have released. Add onion and simmer for a further eight minutes or until the onion is smooth and the mushrooms are lightly browned.

Cook, stirring, for 30 seconds after adding the garlic, thyme, and pepper. Add the soup at this point without dilution and heat thoroughly. Add the chicken, broccoli, and squash after gently tossing everything together. Spread the mixture evenly among the prepared baking plates, then top each one with 1/4 cup Cheddar. Wrap with foil. One dish should be labeled and frozen for up to a month. The final dish should bake for around 25 minutes or until bubbling. Remove the lid and bake for a further 10 to 15 minutes, or until the sides are lightly browned. 10 minutes should pass before serving.

Nutritional value per serving: 109 calories, 3.9 grams of fat, 148 milligrams of sodium, 16 grams of carbohydrates, 1 gram of sugar, 2 grams of fiber, and 2 grams of protein in a single serving (one cup).

26.   *Eggplant Tortillas Casserole*

Serving Size: 8

Preparation time: 1 hour, 10 minutes

Ingredients:

- 1 small eggplant (about 1 lb.)

- Divided 2 teaspoons of canola oil

- Two medium onions, cut thinly

- 3 minced garlic cloves

- 1 teaspoon of chili powder

- Two tablespoons dried oregano

- 1 teaspoon of onion powder

- 1 teaspoon cumin powder

- 1 (28 ounce) can of diced tomatoes without salt

- 2 rinsed, 15-ounce cans of no-salt-added black beans

- 2 cans of mild green chilies, each 4.5 ounces

- 1/4 cup freshly chopped cilantro

- 10 quartered corn tortillas

- 1 cup of extra-sharp Cheddar cheese, shredded

Directions:

Set oven to 375 degrees Fahrenheit. Apply cooking spray to an 8-inch square baking dish and a large rimmed baking sheet. Slice the peeled eggplant into rounds that are 1/4 inch thick. the matches in half (or quarter, if massive). Place a single layer on the baking sheet that has been prepared and brush with 1 Tbsp. over the eggplant with oil. Bake for 10 to 15 minutes, flipping the eggplant once, until the edges start to brown. Cool down. Heat the final tablespoon. oil over medium-high heat in a large nonstick skillet. Add the onions and stir while cooking for about 10 minutes, or until tender. Add the garlic, cumin, onion powder, chili powder, oregano, and keep cooking until aromatic, about 30 seconds. Add tomatoes, beans, chilies, and cilantro after stirring. Place aside. To assemble the casseroles, place a quarter of the tortilla portions on the bottom of each baking dish. Over each tortilla, spread 1 cup of the tomato-bean mixture and top with 1/4 cup Cheddar. 12 of the eggplant portions should be layered on top of each, followed by 1 cup of the tomato-bean mixture. After dividing the remaining tortillas and tomato-bean mixture among the casseroles, top each with 1/4 cup of Cheddar. Each dish should have foil on it. One soup should be labelled and frozen for up to a month. The final casserole should bake for 30 minutes or until bubbling. Remove the lid and continue baking for an additional 10 minutes or until the cheese is lightly browned.

Nutritional value per serving: 113 calories, 3 grams of fat, 123 milligrams of sodium, 46 grams of carbohydrates, 1 gram of sugar, 5 grams of fiber, and 7 grams of protein in a single serving (one cup).

27.   *Enchilada Casserole*

Serving Size: 6

Preparation time: 40 minutes

Ingredients:

• Olive oil, 2 teaspoons

• 1 cup corn kernels, either fresh or frozen

• 1/2 cup green bell peppers, diced

• 1/2 cup red bell peppers, diced

• 1/2 cup onion, diced

• 1 box of 5-ounce baby spinach

• 2 1/2 cups of cooked, shredded chicken breast

• 1 8-ounce pouch of Frontera red or green enchilada sauce

• 1 14 cups freshly made salsa

• Cut eight 1-inch-thick strips from eight 5- or 6-inch corn tortillas.

• 1 1/2 cups of reduced-fat Cheddar cheese, shredded

• 1 cup of grape tomatoes, roughly chopped

• 1/4 cup freshly chopped cilantro

• 14 cup radishes sliced into matchsticks

Directions:

Set the oven to 350°F. In a sizable ovenproof skillet, such cast iron, heat the oil. Add the corn, red and green peppers, and onion; simmer for 7 to 10 minutes, turning regularly, until charred. Add the spinach gradually in batches and simmer, frequently stirring, until wilted, about 1 to 2 minutes.

Chicken, enchilada sauce, and salsa are added and mixed. Add tortilla strips and toss lightly. grate some cheese on top. Place in the oven, and bake for 15 minutes, or until bubbling. Tomatoes, cilantro, and radishes are placed on top of the casserole.

Nutritional value per serving: 237 calories, 4.8 grams of carbs, 1 gram of fiber, 2.1 grams of sugar, 7 grams of fat, 101 mg of cholesterol, 235 mg of sodium, and 32 grams of protein.

28.   *Smoked Turkey And Kale Rice*

Serving Size: 6

Preparation time: 40 minutes

Ingredients:

• Extra virgin olive oil, 1 teaspoon

• 2 cups of leeks, only the white and light green portions, thinly sliced.

• 1 cup of celery, thinly sliced

• 4 cups of kale leaves, sliced

• 1 can of chopped tomatoes, 28 ounces

• 1 cup cottage cheese that is minimal in fat and salt.

• 1 cup quick-cooking or instant brown rice

• 6 ounces of chopped smoked tofu or turkey breast (1 1/2 cups of)

14 cup of water

• One tablespoon of freshly ground pepper, or as desired

• 1 cup of extra-sharp Cheddar cheese, shredded

Directions:

In a sizable, oven-safe skillet, heat the oil over medium-high heat. Dinner should be prepared with leeks and celery, frequently stirring until softening, 2 to 3 minutes. Add the kale and tomatoes, then cook while stirring for one to two minutes, or until the kale begins to wilt. Rice, cottage cheese, water, pepper, and turkey (or tofu) should all be combined. Simmer for a while. Set the heat to medium-low, cover the area, and cook dinner for 10 minutes.

Meanwhile, role rack in higher 1/3 of oven; preheat broiler. Stir the rice mixture, boom the warmth to medium and prepare dinner, uncovered, till a maximum of the liquid has evaporated, 10 to twelve minutes. Spread cheese on top. Broil till the cheese is bubbling, 2 to a few minutes.

Nutritional value per serving: 369 calories, 27 grams of carbohydrates, 2 grams of sugars, 2 grams of fiber, 10 grams of fat, 400 milligrams of sodium, and 37 grams of protein.

29.   *Minestrone*

Serving Size: 8

Preparation time: 6 hours, 30 minutes

Ingredients:

- 4 large carrots, peeled and chopped
- 3 stalks celery, chopped
- 1 small red onion, chopped
- 3 cloves garlic, minced
- 2 cup of fresh green beans, trimmed and cut into 2-inch pieces
- 2 (15 ounce) cans no-sodium-added red kidney beans, rinsed
- 2 (15 ounce) cans no-sodium-added diced tomatoes, undrained
- 6 cup of no-sodium-added vegetable broth, such as Kitchen Basics
- 2 Tsp Italian seasoning
- 1 Tbsp crushed red pepper
- ¾ Tbsp salt, divided
- ½ Tbsp ground pepper
- 1 large zucchini, chopped
- 4 ounces whole-wheat pasta elbows or other small pasta (about 1 cup)
- ½ cup freshly grated Parmesan cheese

Directions:

In a 6- to 8-qt slow cooker, combine the ingredients: carrots, celery, onion, garlic, green beans, kidney beans, tomatoes, broth, Italian seasoning, crushed red pepper, 1/4 tsp salt, and pepper. Cook on Low for 6 to 8 hours with the cover on.

Add the pasta, zucchini, and final 1/2 teaspoon of salt. For 15 to 20 minutes, simmer the pasta on Low with the cover on. Serve immediately, adding roughly 1 1/2 teaspoons of Parmesan to each portion.

Nutritional value per serving: 237 calories, 4.8 grams of carbs, 1 gram of fiber, 2.1 grams of sugar, 7 grams of fat, 101 mg of cholesterol, 235 mg of sodium, and 32 grams of protein.

30.   *Chile Chicken And Tortilla Rice*

Serving Size: 9   **Preparation time:** 9 hours, 50 minutes

Ingredients:

• Nonstick cooking spray

• 1 pound tomatillos, outer husks removed, rinsed

• 1 Tbsp vegetable oil

• ½ cup onion, chopped

• 1 fresh poblano chile pepper, seeded and chopped

• ¼ cup snipped fresh cilantro

• 1 Tbsp sugar

• ½ Tbsp ground cumin

• ¼ Tbsp salt

• 12 (6 inch) corn tortillas, halved

• 3 cup of shredded, cooked chicken breast meat

• 1 ¾ cup of shredded reduced-fat Mexican-style four cheese blend (7 ounces)

• 1 (16 ounce) jar salsa

• 1 Chopped tomato, chopped onion, sliced fresh jalapeño chile peppers, sliced green onion, and snipped fresh cilantro

Directions:

Preheat broiler. Lightly coat a 2-quart square baking dish with cooking spray; set apart. Line a 15x10x1-inch baking pan with foil. Place tomatillos withinside the baking pan. Broil four to 5 inches from the warmth for six to eight mins or till softened and charred, turning occasionally. Set apart to cool slightly. In a big skillet heat oil over medium heat.

Add onion and poblano chile pepper; cook and stir for four to 5 minutes or till soft and onion starts to brown.

In a blender or food processor combine tomatillos, onion mixture, cilantro, sugar, cumin and salt. Cover and blend or method till smooth, preventing and scraping down sides as necessary. Spread ¾ cup of the tomatillo aggregate withinside the organized baking dish. Arrange six of the tortilla halves over the tomatillo aggregate, overlapping slightly. Mix 1 cup of the chicken, half a cup of the cheese, and ½ the salsa, spreading evenly.

Add six more tortilla halves and pinnacle with 1 cup chicken, half cup cheese, and ½ of the final tomatillo aggregate, spreading evenly. Add six extra tortilla halves, the last 1 cup of chicken, and the final tomatillo aggregate. Top with the final six tortilla halves and the final salsa, spreading to cowl completely.

Cover the dish with plastic wrap and relax for at least eight hours or as much as 24 hours. Cover and rest the final 3/four cup cheese till needed. Preheat oven to 375 levels F. Remove plastic wrap. Cover dish with foil and bake for forty mins. Remove foil, then sprinkle with the final 3/four cup cheese. Bake roughly 20 mins additional or till cooked through. 10 minutes should pass before serving. Add chopped tomato, onion, jalapeño, inexperienced onion, and/or fresh cilantro as a garnish.

Nutritional value per serving: 88 calories, 9g of carbohydrates, 1g of fiber, 2g of sugar, 4.2g of protein, 2.8g of fat, 15mg of cholesterol, and 140mg of sodium make up the meal.

Desserts

1. Churros

Serving Size: 4

Preparation time: 10 minutes

Ingredients:

- 1 1/2 teaspoons of baking soda
- 1 Egg
- One-half cup of mozzarella cheese
- One cup of almond flour
- Two tablespoons heavy cream
- 2 oz. cheese, cream
- 2 tablespoons of Swerve sugar replacement for confections
- 1/2 tsp. cinnamon

For the garnish:

- 1 Tbsp. Butter (melted)
- 1/2 tsp. cinnamon
- Two tablespoons of granulated Swerve sweetener

Directions:

350 degrees Fahrenheit should be the preheated temperature of your air fryer.

In a bowl that can be heated in the microwave, combine the cream cheese and mozzarella cheese. Microwave for about 30 seconds, or until the cheese is completely melted and combined into a dough. Mix the melted cheese mixture with the baking powder, almond flour, sugar, and 1/2 tsp. cinnamon. Incorporate the egg and heavy whipping cream into the dough mixture. Ensure that it goes smoothly. The dough should be placed in a piping bag or other device with a star-shaped decorator tip.

In the air fryer tray, place the dough strips. Churro sticks should be cooked in the air fryer until the edges are browned (about 4-5 minutes) Melted butter should be brushed on top of the fried churros. In a bowl, combine 1 tsp. of cinnamon and the granulated sugar. The cinnamon should be sprinkled on the buttery air-fried churro sticks.

Nutritional value per serving: Carbohydrate content per serving (4 churros): 4.

2. Chocolate Chips for Keto

Serving Size: 12

Preparation time: 6 minutes

Ingredients:

- A teaspoon of vanilla extract

- 1/2 a cup of coconut flour

- 12 cups of butter

- 1/3 cup of cream cheese

- A third cup of sugar-free chocolate chips

- 1 egg (beaten)

- 1/3 cup of erythritol

Directions:

In a bowl, mix together the butter and cream cheese. Add vanilla extract and erythritol while continuing to whip until foamy. Add the egg and continue beating until incorporated. Coconut flour and chocolate chips should be added. Allow the dough to rest for 10 minutes.

Using a scoop of dough around the size of a tablespoon, shape the cookies. In the basket of the air fryer, bake cookies for 6 minutes.

Add whipped cream, ice cream, or whatever else sounds nice as a topping!

Nutritional value per serving: 138, sodium is 99 mg, sugar is 1 g, fiber is 2 g, cholesterol is 39 mg, fat is 11 g, protein is 2 g, and carbohydrates are 5.8 g per serving (1 g).

3. Bites of Cheesecake

Serving Size: 2

Preparation time: 10 minutes

Ingredients:

• 50 g of almond flour

• Half a cup of erythritol

• 8 oz. cheese, cream

• 4 tablespoons divided heavy cream

erythritol, 2 tablespoons

• 1/8 teaspoon of vanilla extract

Directions:

Cream cheese needs about 20 minutes to soften on the counter. Blend the softened cream cheese, vanilla, heavy cream, and 1/2 cup erythritol until smooth. When the mixture is set, freeze it for about 30 minutes.

In a bowl, combine almond flour and 2 tablespoons of erythritol. Cream the cream cheese that has been frozen.

Roll in the mixture of almond flour. At least two minutes should be spent air frying at 300 degrees Fahrenheit.

Nutritional value per serving: Calories are 82, fat is 6 g, carbohydrates are 2 g, fiber is 0 g, protein is 2 g, sugar is 1 g, and sodium is 49 mg per serving.

4. Sugar-Free Brownies

Serving Size: 6

Preparation time: 35 minutes

Ingredients:

• A quarter cup of Truvia or another sweetener

• One cup of Butter

• 1/2 cup chocolate chips without added sugar

• 3 Eggs

• 1 tsp. vanilla extract

Directions:

In a bowl suitable for the microwave, melt the chocolate and butter for about a minute. Remove and thoroughly whisk the mixture. The sweetener, eggs, and vanilla should be thoroughly blended until fluffy.

In a bowl, combine the combined mixture with the butter and chocolate that have been melted. The mixture should be well-incorporated and even after being beaten.

Place the mixture in the air fryer's basket after adding it to the pan. 350°F for approximately 35 minutes when air frying.

Nutritional value per serving: Calories in a serving are 219; carbohydrates are 2.9g; protein is 3g; fat is 22g; and fiber is 1g.

5. *Tea Cake With Gingerbread*

Serving Size: 15

Preparation time: 1 hour, 15 minutes

Ingredients:

- 2 1/3 cups all-purpose flour

- 1 1/2 tablespoons baking powder

- 1 teaspoon ginger powder

- 1 teaspoon cinnamon powder

- 1/2 tsp of baking soda

- 1/4 cup salt

- 1/4 teaspoon ground cloves

- 1/2 cup of canola oil

- A mixture of sugar substitutes or 1/4 cup of granulated sugar, whichever is greater (see Tip)

- A quarter cup of cold water

- 2.3 cups of full-flavored molasses

- 2 lightly beaten eggs or 12 cup thawed, chilled, or frozen egg product

- Dusting with confectioners' sugar

- Garnishing with fresh raspberries

Directions:

Set the oven to 350 degrees. Prepare a baking pan measuring 13x9x2 inches by lightly spraying it with nonstick cooking spray. Combine the flour, baking powder, ginger, cinnamon, baking soda, salt, and cloves in a medium basin; set aside.

Oil and sugar should be whisked together until well incorporated in a large bowl. Whisk in the eggs, molasses, and bloodless water after adding them. Immediately add the saved flour mixture to the water mixture and whisk until smooth. Dispense into a prepared pan. 45 minutes of baking time, or until a wooden toothpick inserted close to the center of the cake comes out clean. Definitely cool on a twine rack. If desired, top the peak with confectioners' sugar and garnish with raspberries.

Nutritional value per serving: calories 120, sodium is 40 mg, sugar is 3 g, fiber is 2 g, cholesterol is 39 mg, fat is 8 g, protein is 2 g, and carbohydrates are 8 g per serving (1 g).

6. *Delicious Sugar Cookies*

Serving Size: 48

Preparation time: 1 hour

Ingredients:

- 12 cup softened butter
- 4 ounces softened cream cheese
- 1 3/4 cups sugar (see Tips)
- Baking soda, 1 tablespoon
- One tablespoon cream of tartar

- 1/8 tsp. salt
- Three egg yolks
- 12 teaspoon vanilla
- One-quarter cup of all-purpose flour
- 1/2 cup whole-wheat white flour

Directions:

Set the oven to 300 degrees Fahrenheit. Using an electric mixer set to medium to high speed, combine the butter and cream cheese in a large mixing basin for 30 seconds. Salt, baking soda, cream of tartar, and sugar should be added. Beat the mixture until it is well-combined, sometimes scraping the bowl's sides. Vanilla and egg yolks are blended in. Use the mixer to incorporate as much white whole wheat flour and all-purpose flour as you can. Use a wooden spoon to stir in the remaining flour.

Roll the dough into 1-inch diameter balls. Place balls on ungreased cookie sheets 2 inches apart.

Bake for 14 to 16 minutes, or until the edges are firm; do not let the edges brown during this time. On the baking sheet, cool cookies for one minute. Move the cookies to a wire rack to cool.

Nutritional value per serving: Calories are 82, fat is 6 g, carbohydrates are 2 g, fiber is 0 g, protein is 2 g, sugar is 1 g, and sodium is 49 mg per serving.

7. Flourless Choco-Cookies

Serving Size: 16

Preparation time: 40 minutes

Ingredients:

- 1 cup of sugar for confections

- 1/4 cup bittersweet cocoa powder

- 1/8 tsp. salt

- Two big egg whites

- A teaspoon of vanilla extract

- 1/2 cup chopped bittersweet chocolate chunks or chips

Directions:

The oven to 350 degrees Fahrenheit. Use parchment paper to line 2 large baking sheets. Spritz some cooking spray on the paper.

In a medium bowl, mix salt, cocoa powder, and confectioners' sugar. Egg whites are beaten with an electric mixer until smooth peaks form in a large mixing basin. Include vanilla. Using a rubber spatula, fold the cocoa powder mixture inside out until thoroughly combined. Combine with chocolate chips (or chunks).

On the prepared baking sheets, drop the batter by Tspfuls, spacing each cookie by about 2 inches. Bake one sheet at a time for 12 to 14 minutes, or until the tops of the cookies begin to break. Before moving to a twine rack to totally cool, let the pan barely cool.

Nutritional value per serving: 88 calories, 9g of carbohydrates, 1g of fiber, 2g of sugar, 4.2g of protein, 2.8g of fat, 15mg of cholesterol, and 140mg of sodium

8. *Apple Crumble With Oatmeal*

Serving Size: 6

Preparation time: 1 hour

Ingredients:

- 1/2 cup of normal rolled oats

- Two teaspoons of whole-wheat pastry flour

- 2 tsp. brown sugar in a bag

- 1/2 tsp. cinnamon powder

- 1 teaspoon of cold, chopped butter

- Cut three medium Golden Delicious apples into thin wedges after coring them.

- Water, 2 teaspoons

- Fresh lemon juice, 1 teaspoon

- 1 tsp. brown sugar in a bag (see Tips)

- 1 (8-ounce) carton of low-fat vanilla yogurt or frozen yogurt

Directions:

Set the oven to 350 degrees. Combine the oats, flour, 2 teaspoons of brown sugar, and cinnamon in a medium bowl. With a fork, mix everything. Add the butter and stir the mixture with a pastry blender, fork, or your fingers until clumps begin to form.

Toss the apples in a large dish with the water, lemon juice, and last teaspoon of brown sugar. Place the apple mixture in a 9-inch pie pan. The oat mixture should be liberally sprinkled over the apples. Bake for 45 minutes, or until the apples are soft and the topping is brown. Yogurt may be served hot if preferred.

Nutritional value per serving: Calories are 82, fat is 6 g, carbohydrates are 2 g, fiber is 0 g, protein is 2 g, sugar is 1 g, and sodium is 49 mg per serving.

9. Brownies Cookies

Serving Size: 24

Preparation time: 1 hour, 40 minutes

Ingredients:

- 1 cup regular flour
- 1/4 teaspoon baking soda
- 1/4 cup butter.
- 2.3 cups of granulated sugar
- 1/3 cup bittersweet cocoa powder

- 1/4 cup brown sugar in a bag
- 1/4 cup sour milk or buttermilk (see Tip)
- 1 teaspoon vanilla
- Cooking oil nonstick
- Sifted sugar, 1 teaspoon

Directions:

Flour and baking soda should be combined in a small bowl before setting it aside. Butter should melt in a medium pot; remove from heat. Add brown sugar, cocoa powder, and granulated sugar after stirring. Add vanilla and buttermilk and stir. Add the flour aggregate and mix well. For one hour, kick back the dough under cover. (The dough could be hard.)

Set the oven to 350 degrees. Cookie sheets can be lined with parchment paper or lightly sprayed with nonstick cooking spray. Utilizing rounded Tbsps, drop cooled dough onto a cookie sheet.

Until the edges are firm, bake for eight to ten minutes. Cool for one minute on cookie sheet. After transferring, let the chord rack cool. Add some sugar powder to the dish.

Nutritional value per serving: calories 120, sodium is 40 mg, sugar is 3 g, fiber is 2 g, cholesterol is 39 mg, fat is 8 g, protein is 2 g, and carbohydrates are 8 g per serving (1 g).

10. Spiced Cookies With Pumpkin

Serving Size: 36

Preparation time: 1 hour, 15 minutes

Ingredients:

- a third cup of whole-wheat pastry flour

- 2.3 cups of all-purpose flour

- 1 tablespoon baking soda

- 1/2 tsp of baking soda

- 1/2 tsp. salt

- 1 teaspoon cinnamon powder

- 1/2 tsp. ginger powder

- 1/4 tablespoon ground allspice

- 1/4 tablespoon of freshly grated nutmeg

- Two big eggs

- 1/3 cup of Splenda Sugar Blend for Baking or 3/4 cup of packed light brown sugar (see Tips)

- 3/4 cup of canned pumpkin puree without seasoning

- 1/4 cup of canola oil

- 1/4 cup molasses, dark

Directions:

Set the oven to 350 degrees. Apply cooking spray to three baking sheets.

In a large basin, combine the whole-wheat flour, all-purpose flour, baking powder, baking soda, salt, cinnamon, ginger, allspice, and nutmeg. In a second bowl, thoroughly combine the eggs, brown sugar (or Splenda), pumpkin, oil, and molasses. Mix the dry ingredients thoroughly after adding the raisins and the moist ingredients. Stage Tspfuls of the batter should be dropped onto the prepared baking sheets, with the cookies being spaced 1.5 inches apart.

Bake the cookies for 10 to 12 minutes, rotating the baking sheets halfway through, until they are firm to the touch and lightly brown on top. To cool, transfer to a twine rack.

Nutritional value per serving: Calories are 82, fat is 6 g, carbohydrates are 2 g, fiber is 0 g, protein is 2 g, sugar is 1 g, and sodium is 49 mg per serving.

11. Peanut Butter Mini Choco Cakes

Serving Size: 4

Preparation time: 45 minutes

Ingredients:

- 1 stick of butter, cut into pieces, plus additional butter for the ramekins.

- Chocolate chips, one cup

- Powdered sugar, 1/2 cup plus additional for topping

- two huge eggs with two yolks

- Pure vanilla extract, 1 teaspoon

- Unsweetened cocoa powder, 1/4 cup

- All-purpose flour, 1/4 cup

- Kosher salt, 1/2 teaspoon

- Peanut butter, 4 tablespoons

- water, 1 cup

Directions:

4 ramekins should be butter-greased. Melt butter and chocolate chips in a medium microwave-safe bowl in 30-second intervals until smooth. Whisk in the vanilla, egg yolks, powdered sugar, and eggs until well combined. Whisk in the flour, salt, and cocoa powder until just mixed. Only halfway fill the ramekins with batter, cover each with a heaping tablespoon of peanut butter. Add the remaining batter on top. Wrap foil securely around the ramekins. Add water to the Instant Pot after placing the trivet inside. Set three ramekins on the trivet, then place the fourth one in the middle on top. the lid must be locked. Cook for 20 minutes on high. Utilizing tongs, carefully remove the ramekins from the Instant Pot after adhering to the manufacturer's directions for rapid release. Remove the cover and trim the edges with a knife or offset spatula. Before serving, invert onto a dish and sprinkle with confectioner's sugar. 4 ramekins should be butter-greased. Melt butter and chocolate chips in a medium microwave-safe bowl in 30-second intervals until smooth. Whisk in the vanilla, egg yolks, powdered sugar, and eggs until well combined. Whisk in the flour, salt, and cocoa powder until just mixed. Only halfway fill the ramekins with batter, cover each with a heaping tablespoon of peanut butter. Add the remaining batter on top. Wrap foil securely around the ramekins. Remove foil and continue cooking for an additional 6 minutes after 12 minutes at 375°.

Nutritional value per serving: Calories are 82, fat is 6 g, carbohydrates are 2 g, fiber is 0 g, protein is 2 g, sugar is 1 g, and sodium is 49 mg per serving.

12. Tasty Fried Donuts

Serving Size: 6

Preparation time: 2 hours, 4o minutes

Ingredients:

- 1/2 c. milk

- 1 teaspoon of granulated sugar plus 1/4 cup, divided

- Active-dry yeast, 1 (0.25-oz) package or 2 1/4 tsp.

- All-purpose flour, 2 cups

- Kosher salt, 1/2 teaspoon

- 4 tablespoons melted butter

- One big egg

- Pure vanilla extract, 1 teaspoon

Glaze:

- 1 cup of sugar powder

- Pure vanilla extract, 1/2 tsp.

- Unsweetened cocoa powder, 1/4 cup

- 3 tablespoons of milk

Directions:

Spray some frying oil in a big bowl. Add milk to a small glass measuring cup or bowl that can go in the microwave. For 40 seconds, microwave until lukewarm. A teaspoon of sugar should be added, stirred to dissolve, then sprinkled over the yeast and left to stand for 8 minutes or until foamy. Flour and salt should be whipped together in a medium bowl. Whisk the remaining 1/4 cup sugar, butter, egg, and vanilla in a big bowl. Then add the dry ingredients and whisk with a wooden spoon until a shaggy dough forms. Pour in the yeast mixture and swirl to blend. Transfer to a surface that has been lightly dusted with flour, and knead for about 5 minutes, or until the dough is elastic and only slightly tacky. Form into a ball, then put the dough in a basin that has been lightly greased and cover with a fresh dish cloth. Give the dough about an hour to double in size while rising in a warm location. Cooking spray should be used to lightly oil and line a sizable baking sheet. Punch down the dough, then transfer to a lightly dusted work surface and roll into a rectangle that is 1/2 inch thick. Punch out your doughnuts using a doughnut cutter or a 3" and 1" biscuit cutter. Any leftover pieces can be combined and used to create new doughnuts or holes. Doughnuts and holes should be placed on baking pans, covered with a dish towel, and given another 40 to one hour to rise. Cooking spray should be used to grease the air fryer basket before adding 2 doughnuts and 2 doughnut holes at a time, making sure they don't touch. Cook for 6 minutes at 375 degrees until thoroughly browned. Repeat with the remaining dough and place on cooling rack. Doughnuts can be covered in glaze (see recipe below) or coated with cinnamon sugar. After returning, wait five minutes before serving on the cooling rack.

Mix the milk, vanilla, and powdered sugar in a medium bowl until well combined.

Mix the milk, cocoa powder, and powdered sugar in a medium bowl.

Mix sugar and cinnamon together in a sizable shallow bowl. Sprinkle cinnamon sugar and melted butter over the doughnuts.

Nutritional value per serving: Calories are 82, fat is 6 g, carbohydrates are 2 g, fiber is 0 g, protein is 2 g, sugar is 1 g, and sodium is 49 mg per serving.

13. Sugar Free Donuts

Serving Size: 6

Preparation time: 15 minutes

Ingredients:

• 1/2 tsp. of baking powder,

• six tablespoons of unsweetened cocoa powder from Dutch Process, a half teaspoon of baking soda, and

• A single egg,

• Splenda in six tablespoons,

• One cup of all-purpose low-carb flour,

• 3 tablespoons butter,

• One ounce of chocolate that hasn't been sweetened,

• One-fourth cup of plain yogurt.

Directions:

Place all of the dry ingredients in a bowl that is about medium in size and thoroughly stir them together. In a small saucepan, combine the chocolate and butter. Heat the mixture over medium-low heat. until melted, stir. Add the yogurt and egg to the first bowl and stir to combine. Then, add the chocolate and melted butter and whisk to combine. Place the bowl in the refrigerator and let it sit there for 30 minutes. Take the batter out of the fridge, then scoop out just enough with a tablespoon to make doughnut-shaped balls in your palms. Set your air fryer's temperature to 350 degrees and coat the basket gently with nonstick spray.

Nutritional value per serving: 19 calories, 1 gram of carbs, 1 gram of fiber, 1 gram of sugar, 1 gram of protein, 2 gram of fat, 7 milligrams of cholesterol, and 41 milligrams of sodium.

14. Non-Sugary Vanilla Cheesecake

Serving Size: 12

Preparation time: 40 minutes

Ingredients:

• 3 eggs

• 1.5 cups of sugar substitute (I use powdered Swerve Sweetener)

• 1 teaspoon of lemon juice

• 24 ounces of cream cheese at room temperature

• One-half milligrams of vanilla bean powder

• One cup of unsweetened vanilla Greek yogurt

• One tablespoon of vanilla bean paste

Directions:

Combine the eggs and softened cream cheese in a bowl, and stir until the mixture is entirely smooth. Include the Greek yogurt that hasn't been sweetened after blending. Add your sugar substitute and then restart the blending. After blending, add the lemon juice, vanilla juice, and vanilla powder, and blend again until the liquid is completely smooth.

Spray frying spray on the air fryer's included tray. Put the mixture on the tray, and then place the tray in the air fryer's basket. Fry the mixture in an air fryer at 325 degrees Fahrenheit for about 40 minutes, or until the top starts to turn brown.

Nutritional value per serving: 21 grams of fat, 3.8 grams of carbs, 4 grams of protein, 249 calories, 1 gram of fiber, and 2.9 grams of sugar.

15. Lemon Biscuits Without Sugar

Serving Size: 24

Preparation time: 5 minutes

Ingredients:

• 1/2 cup of Swerve granular sweetener;

• a half-teaspoon of baking soda

• 0.5 teaspoons of salt;

• a half-cup of coconut flour

• Lemon juice, 1 tablespoon;

• Two egg yolks

• 1/2 teaspoon liquid stevia with vanilla;

• Melted 1/2 cup unsalted butter is optional.

• One-fourth teaspoon lemon extract

Directions:

Set the air fryer's temperature to 350° Fahrenheit (180 degrees Celsius). Secondly, combine the first four ingredients in a bowl. Give the mixture a thorough stir to make sure there are no large clumps remaining.

Beat the butter in a stand mixer equipped with a paddle attachment until it has a very creamy texture. Then, combine the ingredients by beating the mixture on the slowest speed while adding the egg yolks, vanilla extract, lemon essence, and lemon juice. The batter must be positioned in the center of a sizable sheet of plastic wrap that has been spread out on the counter. Use the above process to form the wrap into a log after rolling it over the dough and removing any extra. Wrap firmly and keep in the fridge for a minimum of a couple hours or all day.

Spread grease all over the air fryer's basket. Slice cookies from the bottom half of the log after removing the wrapper and cutting them to a thickness of 14 inches. The leftover batter needs to be refrigerated after usage. Place as many cookie slices in a single layer as you can in the air fryer's basket. For three to five minutes, bake the cookies. After the cookies have cooled for two minutes in the basket, they can be taken out and allowed to complete cooling on a wire rack. Use the leftover dough to repeat the process. After the cake has cooled, cover it with some icing and serve.

Nutritional value per serving: 5 grams of fat, 31 milligrams of cholesterol, 111 milligrams of sodium, 2 grams of carbs, 1 gram of fiber, 1 gram of sugar, 1 gram of protein, 64 calories.

16. Dip- Banana Pancakes

Serving Size: 1

Preparation time: 15 minutes

Ingredients:

- 3 bananas, cut in half and longitudinally sliced

- 10 grams of butter

- 1 batch of pancake batter was made (see below)

- melted chocolate that can be dipped

- All-purpose flour, 1 1/2 cups

- Baking powder, 1 tablespoon

- Packet brown sugar, two tablespoons

- kosher salt, 1 teaspoon

- Milk, 3/4 cup, whole

- 0.5 cups of sour cream

- two huge eggs

- Pure vanilla extract, 1 teaspoon

Directions:

Mix the flour, baking soda, brown sugar, and salt in a big bowl. Whisk the milk, sour cream, and eggs in a separate bowl before adding each egg one at a time. Add vanilla and stir. With a wooden spoon, mix the dry ingredients after adding the wet ones.

Dip bananas in pancake batter in a big bowl. Melt butter in a large skillet over a low heat. Add the dipped bananas and fry for 2 minutes on each side, or until golden.

For dipping, serve with melted chocolate. Cooking spray should be used to oil and parchment paper the air fryer basket. Put bananas on parchment paper in a single layer after dipping them in pancake batter in batches. 16 minutes of cooking, 350° until golden.

For dipping, serve with melted chocolate.

Nutritional value per serving: 21 grams of fat, 3.8 grams of carbs, 4 grams of protein, 249 calories, 1 gram of fiber, and 2.9 grams of sugar.

17. Peanut Butter Cookies

Serving Size: 8

Preparation time: 10 minutes

Ingredients:

• 1 cup artificial sweetener

• 1 teaspoon stevia liquid drops

• 1 egg (beaten)

• One cup of organic peanut butter

Directions:

Combine the ingredients to form a dough. Create 24 balls out of the dough. Press the balls onto a cutting board or cookie sheet using the fork. The fork will assist in forming a crisscross pattern on the dough's surface. Place the cookies in the basket after arranging them on the air fryer tray. Cook the cookies in the air for at least 10 minutes at 325 degrees Fahrenheit. Let the cookies cool completely before consuming.

Nutritional value per serving: 201 calories, 6g of carbohydrates, 10g of protein, 15g of fat, 18mg of cholesterol, 9mg of sodium, 9g of fiber, and 1.9g of sugar.

18. Barbecued Peaches

Serving Size: 6

Preparation time: 8 minutes

Ingredients:

• 2 teaspoons maple syrup

• Grilling oils (optional)

• 2 tablespoons chopped walnuts

• Three ripe peaches (cut in half and pitted)

• Ice cream (optional)

Directions:

Place the peach in the air fryer skin side down and pour with maple syrup. Cook for 8 to 12 minutes at 350°F. Add ice cream and chopped walnuts before serving.

Nutritional value per serving: 59 calories, 7 grams of carbohydrates, 1 gram of fiber, 6 grams of sugar, 3 grams of fat, and 1 milligram of sodium

19. Sugar-Free Pound Cake

Serving Size: 8

Preparation time: 20 minutes

Ingredients:

• 1 cup and 2 tablespoons sugar substitute (I use Splenda)

• 1-and-a-half cups low-carb all-purpose flour

• 0.5 cups Butter (at room temperature)

• 4 Eggs

• 1/2 teaspoon of baking soda

• A teaspoon of vanilla extract

Directions:

Set the air fryer's temperature to 350°F. Use pre-cut parchment paper or oil to prepare the cake pan. Combine the baking powder and low-carb flour in a bowl.

Use a different bowl to combine butter and sugar substitute. Add the eggs one at a time, giving each addition a gentle swirl. Next, include the vanilla extract. Stir the butter into the flour mixture just until incorporated. If it appears overly thick, add an additional teaspoon, or more, of heavy whipping cream or similar dairy product. Pour the batter into the prepared cake pan. In the air fryer, put the pan.

Bake the cake for 15-20 minutes, or until a toothpick inserted in the middle comes out clean. Allow the cake to cool completely before removing it from the pan.

Nutritional value per serving: 234 calories; 19g of carbohydrates; 1g of fiber; 1g of sugar; 5g of protein; 13g of fat; 109 mg of cholesterol; 141 mg of sodium.

20. Crunchy Cinnamon Rolls

Serving Size: 6

Preparation time: 30 minutes

Ingredients:

- 2 tablespoons of melted butter plus more for brushing

- Packet brown sugar, one-third cup

- Ground cinnamon, half a teaspoon

- Halal salt

- universal flour, for surfaces

- 1 tube (8 oz.) of chilled Crescent rolls

- 2 oz. softened cream cheese

- Powdered sugar, half a cup

- whole milk, plus more, if necessary, 1 tablespoon

Directions:

Form rolls: Butter should be used to line the parchment paper on the air fryer's bottom. Mix the butter, brown sugar, cinnamon, and a generous amount of salt in a medium bowl until well-combined and fluffy. Crescent rolls should be rolled out in one piece on a lightly dusted surface. Together with a pinch, fold the seams in half. Make a 9" x 7" rectangle by rolling. Over the dough, spread the butter mixture, leaving a 1/4-inch border. Roll the dough up like a jelly roll, starting at one long edge, and cut into six pieces crosswise.

Place the prepared food in the air fryer, cut-side up and equally spaced. Set the air fryer to 350 degrees and cook for 10 minutes, or until golden and thoroughly done. Creating the glaze Cream cheese, powdered sugar, and milk should be combined in a medium bowl. If required, add a teaspoon at a time more milk to thin glaze.

Nutritional value per serving: 299 calories, 4 g protein, 40 g carbohydrates, .15 g fiber, 26 g sugar, 15 g fat, g saturated fat, 385 mg sodium.

21. *Fried Quesitos*

Serving Size: 18

Preparation time: 25 minutes

Ingredients:

- 250g pack of chopped cream cheese

- 2 tbsp of pure icing sugar plus more for dusting

- 1 teaspoon vanilla extract

- 2 freshly defrosted sheets of frozen butter puff pastry

- 1 gently whisked egg

- purchased caramel sauce and served (optional)

Directions:

Mash the cream cheese in a bowl using a fork. Vanilla and icing sugar are added. Up until smooth, mix with a spatula.

Each pastry sheet should be cut into 9 squares. Either pastry square should have 2 teaspoonfuls of the mixture spread across it diagonally, leaving a 1.5 cm gap at each end.

One pastry square's diagonal corner should be folded over the mixture. Gently fold and push the top corner of the opposite side, fixing if necessary with a small amount of egg. Apply egg to pastry. Repeat with the remaining pastry, egg, and mixture.

Oil a basket for an air fryer sparingly. Quesitos should be cooked in batches and spaced 2 cm apart in a basket at 180°C for 10 to 12 minutes, or until golden (see tip). Put on a wire rack to cool a little.

If using caramel sauce, spread it over the quesitos and sprinkle them with more icing sugar. Serve hot.

Nutritional value per serving: 59 calories, 7 grams of carbohydrates, 1 gram of fiber, 6 grams of sugar, 3 grams of fat, and 1 milligram of sodium

22.   *Chocolate And Fudge Pudding*

Serving Size: 8

Preparation time: 55 minutes

Ingredients:

• Half a cup of whole wheat pastry flour (see Ingredient notes)

• Half a cup of all-purpose flour

• For baking, use 1/3 cup sugar or 3 teaspoons Splenda Sugar Blend (see Ingredient notes)

• Sifted 1/4 cup of unsweetened cocoa powder

• 1 1/2 tablespoons baking powder

• 1/2 tsp. salt

• 1 big egg

• 1/2 cup of 1% milk

• Canola oil, 2 teaspoons

• Two tablespoons vanilla extract

• 3/4 cup chocolate chips, semisweet (optional)

• A hot, freshly prepared cup of coffee

• 1/3 cup packed light brown sugar or Granular Splenda

• 1/4 cup toasted, chopped walnuts or pecans

• Confectioners' sugar, used as dust

Directions:

Oven to 350 degrees Fahrenheit. Spray cooking oil in a 1 1/2 to 2-quart baking dish. In a sizable basin, combine the whole-wheat flour, all-purpose flour, sugar (or Splenda Sugar Blend), cocoa, baking powder, and salt. In a tumbler measuring cup, whisk together the egg, milk, oil, and vanilla. Add to the flour mixture and incorporate by mixing with a rubber spatula. If using, fold in the chocolate chips. Pour the batter into the baking pan that has been prepared. Brown sugar (or Splenda Granular) and warm coffee should be combined inside the measuring cup before being poured over the batter. Add some nuts on top. (At this point, it may also appear strange; do not worry. Cake office work on the pinnacle with sauce underneath while it is baking.)

Bake the pudding cake for 30 to 35 minutes, or until the pinnacle springs begin to lightly touch. Allow to cool for at least 10 minutes. Serve warm or warm, with confectioners' sugar on top.

Nutritional value per serving: 21 grams of fat, 3.8 grams of carbs, 4 grams of protein, 249 calories, 1 gram of fiber, and 2.9 grams of sugar.

23. Raisins And Cinnamon Cookies

Serving Size: 24

Preparation time: 1 hour, 15 minutes

Ingredients:

- 1 cup whole-wheat white flour

- 1 tablespoon baking soda

- 1 teaspoon cinnamon powder

- 1/2 tsp. salt

- 2.3 cups of light brown sugar in bags

- 6 tablespoons melted unsalted butter

- 1 big egg

- 1 1/2 teaspoons of vanilla extract

- 1 cup rolled old-fashioned oats

- 1/2 cup of raisins

Directions:

Set the oven to 350°F. Apply cooking spray sparingly to a baking sheet. In a larger basin, stir together the flour, baking powder, cinnamon, and salt.

In a big basin, combine sugar, butter, egg, and vanilla. Oats, raisins, and flour mixture should be added and thoroughly blended with a wooden spoon. Drop one-tenth of a teaspoon of batter onto the prepared baking sheet to make 12 cookies each batch. Bake for 12 to 14 minutes, or until the bottom is golden brown. Prior to moving to a wire rack to thoroughly cool, let the baked goods cool on the baking sheet for 5 minutes. Continue with the final batter.

Nutritional value per serving: 234 calories; 19g of carbohydrates; 1g of fiber; 1g of sugar; 5g of protein; 13g of fat; 109 mg of cholesterol; 141 mg of sodium.

24. *Apple Squares*

Serving Size: 16

Preparation time: 1 hour

Ingredients:

- 1 1/2 cups of regular flour
- 1 cup oats, old-fashioned
- 1 cup of light brown sugar in bags
- 1 tablespoon lemon zest, grated
- 1/4 cup of baking powder
- 1/2 tsp. salt

- 1/2 tsp. cinnamon powder
- 1/4 teaspoon ground nutmeg
- 3 teaspoons canola oil
- Thawed 1/4 cup apple juice concentrate
- 2 medium tart Granny Smith apples, peeled and sliced thinly
- 1/4 cup walnuts, roughly chopped

Directions:

Set the oven to 350°F. Spray cooking spray in a 9-inch square baking pan. In a large bowl, combine the flour, oats, brown sugar, lemon zest, baking soda, salt, cinnamon, and nutmeg. Work together with oil and apple juice using your fingers' sides until crumbly crumbs form.

2 cups of the oat mixture should be pressed firmly into the prepared pan. Over the crust, arrange the apples in three rows. Add walnuts to the final oat mixture. Sprinkle the walnut mixture carelessly over the apples and press down firmly to create an even coating.

Bake for 30 to 35 minutes, or until the top is golden brown and the apples are tender when probed with a sharp knife. On a wire rack, cool, to be honest.

Nutritional value per serving: 299 calories, 4 g protein, 40 g carbohydrates, .15 g fiber, 26 g sugar, 15 g fat, g saturated fat, 385 mg sodium.

25. *Sugar Free Oatmeal Cookies*

Serving Size: 12

Preparation time: 1 hour, 15 minutes

Ingredients:

- 1 cup oats that are quick to cook (see Tip)

- 1/4 cup almond meal or flour

- 1/4 cup cinnamon powder

- 1/4 cup salt

- 2 mashed medium-ripe bananas

- 1/2 cup natural peanut butter or almond butter

- 3/4 cup dates or raisins, chopped

Directions:

Bake at 350 degrees Fahrenheit. Use parchment paper or a silicone baking mat to line a large baking sheet. In a medium bowl, combine the oats, salt, cinnamon, and almond flour (or almond meal). In a large bowl, thoroughly blend vanilla, almond butter (or peanut butter), and bananas. Use a wooden spoon to whisk the banana mixture after adding the dry ingredients and raisins (or dates). Make 12 cookies each batch by rolling or scooping one teaspoon of dough into balls and placing them on the baking sheet that has been prepared. Use a fork to press down and gently flatten.

Bake for about 15 minutes, or until the bottom is moderately browned and firm to the touch. Place on a wire rack to completely unwind. Continue with the final batter.

Nutritional value per serving: 234 calories; 19g of carbohydrates; 1g of fiber; 1g of sugar; 5g of protein; 13g of fat; 109 mg of cholesterol; 141 mg of sodium.

26. *Delicious Choco Cake*

Serving Size: 12

Preparation time: 1 hour

Ingredients:

• 2 teaspoons plus 3/4 cup whole-wheat pastry flour (see Ingredient Note)

• 1/2 cup sugar, granulated

• 1/3 cup bittersweet cocoa powder

• 1 tablespoon baking soda

• Baking soda, 1 tablespoon

• 1/4 cup salt

• 1/2 cup buttermilk without fat (see Tip)

• 1/2 cup of light brown sugar in bags

• One big, lightly beaten egg

• Canola oil, 2 teaspoons

• A teaspoon of vanilla extract

• 1/2 cup hot, strong coffee

• Confectioners' sugar, used as dust

Directions:

Set the oven to 350 degrees. Spray cooking spray in a 9-inch spherical cake pan. Wrap a circle of wax paper around the pan. In a big basin, combine salt, baking soda, baking powder, cocoa, and flour. Buttermilk, brown sugar, egg, oil, and vanilla should all be added. For two minutes, use a medium speed electric mixer. Beat in the hot espresso after adding it. The batter (can be quite thin). Fill the prepared pan with the batter.

Bake the cake for 30 to 35 minutes, or until a skewer inserted in the center comes out clean. After cooling for ten minutes on a wire rack in the pan, remove from the pan, remove the wax paper, and let cool completely. Before cutting, sprinkle confectioners' sugar over the summit.

Nutritional value per serving: Calories are 82, fat is 6 g, carbohydrates are 2 g, fiber is 0 g, protein is 2 g, sugar is 1 g, and sodium is 49 mg per serving.

27. *Mini Oreo Cheesecakes*

Serving Size: 10

Preparation time: 45 minutes

Ingredients:

- 10 Original Oreo cookies

- 250g of room temperature, finely sliced cream cheese

- 1 gently whisked egg

- Mars chocolate bar, 64g pkt (2 packs), chopped

- Sugar icing, for dusting (optional)

Directions:

Line up 10 little patty cases on top of each other. Cookie halves can be separated using a little knife. Put half of the cookie halves into the burger casings with the cream-side up. Cream cheese should be creamy after being beat with electric beaters in a bowl. Add the egg, then mix thoroughly.

Set air fryer to 160C before using. Fill each patty shell with 2 tablespoons of the cream cheese mixture. Add the last of the Oreo halves on top, cream side up. Transfer carefully to the air fryer basket. For 8 minutes or until just set, cook in batches.

Cheesecakes should be moved to a wire rack to cool. Place in the refrigerator to chill for up to overnight. If using, sprinkle gently with icing sugar.

In a bowl that is microwave-safe, put chocolate bars. 45 seconds on high in the microwave, or until softened. until nearly smooth, stir. the mixture of cream cheese. Blend until smooth.

Nutritional value per serving: 234 calories; 19g of carbohydrates; 1g of fiber; 1g of sugar; 5g of protein; 13g of fat; 109 mg of cholesterol; 141 mg of sodium.

28. *Puff Lemon Bars*

Serving Size: 12

Preparation time: 30 minutes

Ingredients:

- 160g (1/2 cup) of lemon curd was purchased.
- Pauls French Vanilla Double Thick Custard, 120g (1/2 cup).
- 2 freshly thawed sheets of frozen puff pastry
- Sugar icing, for dusting
- Lemon rind, finely grated, for serving.

Directions:

In a bowl, combine the custard and lemon curd with a spatula until barely blended.

Slice a pastry sheet in half. To mark out 6 rectangles, lightly score a line down the middle of one half and then 2 crossways. Put 1 tablespoon of the curd mixture in the middle of each rectangle, using the scored lines as a guide.

Place the remaining pastry half over the top with care. To seal, gently press your finger along the borders and between the custard. Into six rectangles, cut. To create 12 bars, repeat with the remaining pastry and filling.

Spray some oil on the air fryer basket's base. Add three or four rectangles to the basket. Cook for five minutes at 180°C. After 3 minutes, flip the bars over and continue cooking until golden and puffy. to a wire rack, transfer. Continue with the additional rectangles.

To serve, sprinkle with lemon rind and icing sugar.

Nutritional value per serving: Calories are 82, fat is 6 g, carbohydrates are 2 g, fiber is 0 g, protein is 2 g, sugar is 1 g, and sodium is 49 mg per serving.

29. *Banana Muffins*

Serving Size: 18

Preparation time: 20 minutes

Ingredients:

- two ripe bananas
- 1 cup of self-raising flour, 150 grams
- Brown sugar, 60g (1/3 cup, loosely packed)
- 1 egg

- Olive oil, 60 ml (1/4 cup).
- 1/4 cup of buttermilk in 60 ml
- Extra (optional) maple syrup to serve along with the syrup to brush

Directions:

Bananas should be mashed with a fork in a small bowl. Set aside until required.

Use a balloon whisk to whisk the flour and sugar in a medium bowl. Make a well in the centre. Add the egg , oil and buttermilk . Use the whisk to break up the egg. Use a wooden spoon to stir until the mixture is mixed. Stir through the banana.

Set an air fryer to 180C before using. Give each of the nine patty cases half of the mixture. Carefully slide the cases to the rack after removing the rack from the air fryer. Put the rack back in the fryer. Cook the muffins for 8 to 10 minutes, or until done. to a wire rack, transfer. To create 18 muffins, repeat the process with the remaining batter.

While the muffins are still warm, drizzle maple syrup over the tops. If desired, drizzle more maple syrup on the servings.

Nutritional value per serving: 21 grams of fat, 3.8 grams of carbs, 4 grams of protein, 249 calories, 1 gram of fiber, and 2.9 grams of sugar.

30. *Fried Ice Cream*

Serving Size: 12

Preparation time: 8 hours, 30 minutes

Ingredients:

- 1.5 liters of premium vanilla ice cream
- 300g crushed plain digestive biscuits
- 3 eggs
- 1 1/2 tbsp milk
- Caramilk sauce
- 180g Cadbury Caramilk chocolate, finely chopped
- 185ml (3/4 cup) thickened cream

Directions:

Place a baking tray in the freezer for 10 minutes to chill.

Line the tray with baking paper. Working rapidly, scoop ice-cream into 12 balls and place on prepared dish. Place in the freezer for 4 hours or until solid. Place the crushed biscuits into a large shallow bowl. Working with one at a time, roll ice-cream balls in the crushed biscuits to coat, shaking off excess. Back in the tray, freeze for one further hour, or until solid.

In a bowl, whisk the milk and eggs together. Roll each ball, one at a time, in the egg mixture, then evenly coat with the remaining broken biscuits. go back to tray. Freeze for a full hour, or until solid. Refrigerate any egg mixture that is left over. To double-coat, repeat coating with the remaining balls, egg mixture, and biscuit crumbs. Overnight in the freezer, until extremely stiff.

Make the Caramilk sauce in the meantime by combining the chocolate and cream in a microwave-safe bowl. Cook for 112 minutes on high, or until chocolate is melted. until smooth, stir. For five minutes, preheat the air fryer at 200°C. Two ice cream balls should be placed on a small baking paper sheet (you need to be able to lift the paper with the ice-cream balls on it, but not so big that it covers the whole base of the air fryer basket). Spray some oil on.

Place into the air fryer and cook at 200°C for 2 minutes. Place the balls on plates for serving. Drizzle with Caramilk sauce and serve immediately.

Nutritional value per serving: 21 grams of fat, 3.8 grams of carbs, 4 grams of protein, 249 calories, 1 gram of fiber, and 2.9 grams of sugar.

Conclusion

If you're struggling with diabetes, a healthy weight loss program may be the best treatment option. With the help of reasonable element manipulation, a diabetic weight reduction program can help you achieve more than simply blood sugar control while still being healthy.

Consequences such as coronary heart disease and cancer are less likely to manifest in those who regularly engage in rigorous fitness routines. Universal fitness and lowering the risk of various fitness issues depend on eating a well-balanced diet.

In addition to helping you maintain a healthy weight and blood sugar levels, a diabetic weight loss program can reduce the amount of medication your body needs, prevent dangerous lows and highs, and increase your metabolism so you have better control over how your body processes food. The customized diabetic diet meal plan is simple to put together.

Yet, at initially, it may seem difficult. Even though you may have to adjust your eating habits and learn to cook for yourself and your family instead of always relying on fast food restaurants, you will be well on your way to enjoying the benefits of a healthy way of life. In this cookbook, you'll find detailed instructions for making a wide variety of dishes. Everything from morning foods through grains, beans, legumes, salads, veggies, meat, seafood, soups, snacks, and desserts may be found here. The recipes and advice in this e-book are great for anyone looking to get started on a diabetic diet and learn how to cook healthy meals from the comfort of their own home. We hope that you'll find this cookbook helpful in your pursuit of a healthier way of life.

It has simple recipes for every type of food imaginable, with possible explanations written in a way that even a child might grasp. Recipes are simple enough that a beginner can make them with no trouble at all. In spite of having diabetes, you still have options in terms of what you can eat. Because food is so essential to survival, we should no longer be limited to flavor combinations we have no control over. There is a wealth of wonderful foods available to you; all you need to do is figure out how to put them together. We also think the protected meal plan is something you should try out, as it may make your trip easier. Changing your eating habits may be challenging, but it is possible. You need drive and determination to actually implement the weight loss plan. Your body will appreciate your care, but that's not all. But it will also reward you by helping you feel more motivated and organized all through the day.

About The Author

Mackenzie Geller came from a wonderful family in Liverpool, England.

Growing up, she discovered a passion for the kitchen. At 19, she uprooted to Copenhagen, where she got a job at a local bakery. As a result, she has prepared a ridiculous number of pies and other delicious goodies since then.

She developed a similar passion for dieting over time. She has found great satisfaction in exploring new tasty but healthy meals that help her stay on the ketogenic diet. She's had plenty of time to try out new flavor combinations, and through trial and error, she's discovered some very spectacular dishes.

Her books contain all of these amazing recipes.

Manufactured by Amazon.ca
Bolton, ON